RAISING FAITHFUL KIDS

This is the Stuff of Faith

Denise Janssen,
Carmichael D. Crutchfield,
Virginia A. Lee,
and Jessica Young Brown,
Editors

Judson Press™

DISTINGUISHED PUBLISHERS SINCE 1824

VALLEY FORGE, PA

Contents

Introduction: Faith Formation in Everyday Life......... 1

Section I: The Power of Ritual 7

1. Faith that Is More *Caught* than Taught... 9
    Jenna Williams
2. Blessing Our Children 12
    Thomas Rawls
3. Music in the Air......................... 14
    Emily Bryant
4. A Parent's Role.......................... 16
    Carmichael D. Crutchfield
5. Learning to Pray from a Kneeling Father 19
    Evelyn L. Parker
6. Serving Children More than Food 22
    Diane Janssen Hemmen
7. Reflections on Parenting from a Religious/
    Christian Educator........................ 24
    Mary A. Love
8. Building Relationships 27
    Keosha Branch
9. It Takes a Faith Community 29
    Willa M. Ross
10. Celebrating Children: Inspiring Congregational
    Vitality................................. 31
    Mary H. Young
11. The Role of the Church in Caregiving 34
    Willa M. Ross

Section II: The Sensory Experience 37

12. Let's Get Messy 39
    Durecia D. Moorer

13. A Grown-up Song 41
    Tamar Wasoian
14. Introducing the Holy Spirit as the True and
    Good Shepherd. 43
    Charis Goodman
15. The Sounds and Shape of Love. 46
    Rachel Pierce
16. Spring Break Rituals. 49
    Barbara Annette Fears
17. When Is God Coming to Houston? 52
    Mai-Anh Le Tran
18. Story of Faith and Children 55
    Cheryle Walters Rodriguez
19. Bedtime Moments of Gratitude 57
    Nicole Brocato

Section III: Storytelling. 59
20. Read to Raise Reflective Kids. 61
    Archana Samuel
21. A Story. 63
    Tamar Wasoian
22. Nurturing Social and Sacred Conversations 65
    Zanique Davis
23. Enjoy the Journey. 68
    Toccoro A. Arrington
24. When Words Get in the Way 70
    Colin McDonald
25. God Is in My Mouth!. 73
    Ashley Prescott Barlow-Thompson

Section IV: Difficult Conversations. 77
26. Connect Before Correct 79
    Amy Howard
27. Emerging Trust. 82
    Randy Creath

Contents

28. "Grandma, I don't want to die!" 85
    Virginia A. Lee
29. Openness 88
    Bethany Wherry
30. Responding to Tough Questions. 91
    Karen-Marie Yust
31. Feeling Big Feelings 93
    Justin Thornburgh
32. A Very Dark Night. 95
    Tamar Wasoian
33. Raising Anti-Racist Children 97
    Paula Cripps-Vallejo
34. Parents Talking about Human Sexuality. 99
    Carmichael D. Crutchfield
35. Instilling Faith as a Caregiver. 101
    Cindy A. Cummins
36. God's Provision of Church Family as
    Extended Family. 104
    Hilary Ohrt
37. Teaching by What We Leave Out 106
    Erin S. Keyes
38. Parenting Through a Pandemic. 109
    Tiffany P. Harris-Greene
39. Navigating Separation and Divorce 111
    Jeffrey A. Howard
40. When Children Are Sick. 113
    Teresa E. Snorton
41. Naming How Faith Impacts Our Choices. 115
    Emily A. Peck
42. Trisagion 118
    Jenny Haddad Mosher

Section V: Loosening Up. 121
43. And a Child Shall Lead Them. 123
    Jessica Young Brown

44. And I'm Way More! 126
    Tamar Wasoian
45. When Mario Came to Church 128
    Denise Janssen
46. A Big Ask to Creatively Form Faith 131
    Amy Howard
47. No More Diapers! 133
    Tamar Wasoian
48. Calming Spaces 136
    Lucas Pepper
49. Being Heard Is Being Loved 138
    Shelley Willmann Weakly
50. Curating Curiosity 140
    Paula Cripps-Vallejo
51. A Dollar that Brings My Family Together. 142
    Jenna Williams
52. Wondering Together. 145
    Melanie Black

Conclusion. 148
Bibliography. 162
Biographical Snapshots of the Contributors of
Reflections in this Book 163

Introduction

Faith Formation in Everyday Life

[You] "might be surprised to know that the single, most powerful causal influence on the religious lives of [children] is the religious lives of their parents [and caregivers]. Not their peers, not the media, not their youth group leader or clergy, not their religious school teachers." And this has not changed in research dating back to the 1970s.[1]

These words from sociologist Christian Smith in his book, *Handing Down the Faith*, echo dozens of studies over the last few decades that came to roughly the same conclusion. The Lilly Endowment took note and provided tens of millions of dollars in funding to projects that build on this research to help caregivers and parents live into their role as their child's primary religious educator.[2] Essentially, even when the children in your life sometimes act as if it is not the case, they still closely observe parents and caregivers, listening to what you say or do (or do not say and do) and drawing upon your values as they form their own. Your faith and values are key to the faith and values that are forming in the lives of the children in your care.

This is a book for parents *and* caregivers. We embrace the reality that families come in many varieties and configurations. This book recognizes that parents, grandparents and great-grandparents, aunts and uncles, foster parents and step-parents, and many, many others fill the role of caregiver in a child's life. The relationships of a family are most important—not the composition. We assume no typical or ideal family in this resource. We celebrate them all! We see you—every kind of caregiver in every kind of family—and we want to support your thriving.

With this in mind, we created *Raising Faithful Kids* to invite you into a conversation about faith formation (broadly defined) and the pivotal role parents and caregivers play in it. The purpose of this resource is to equip parents and caregivers with tools and processes for sharing faith formation. We wrote this book to help you consider the faith and values you hope to share with your children! Many of us have lived with the message that the best way to teach our children faith is to invest our time and energy into consistent engagement in organized religions and faith communities. While we, the editors, certainly believe that engagement in faith communities is vital to our faith experiences, we also believe that what happens at home and in the outside world in our everyday interactions with our kids is a key component of what it means to teach them to live a faithful life.

You may think that faith formation is about responding to big existential questions, and it is. Maybe these theological discussions feel above your education level, pay grade, or expertise. Sometimes, theological educators produce books that seem to be theoretical and without practical application in our local churches or personal lives. This is not that kind of book. In this resource, we invite you to think about the power of all the little moments in your caregiving journey—car rides, mealtimes, and bedtime routines. What opportunities do you have in those tiny moments to tell the big story of what you believe and the kind of person you endeavor to be? You are an expert in your home and with your kids. As such, this volume invites you to step into new and exciting ways of leadership in forming the faith of the children for whom you are responsible. We believe these small interactions are crucial to our caregiving journeys and faith (however we may define it). While we may not remember the details of the interactions years from now, we will be left with a felt sense of our relationships with each other and our connection to the Creator. *This is the stuff of faith.* Such interactions form the material we use to tackle the big theological questions that may sometimes seem outside our grasp.

A striking number of the reflections in this resource invite you into a posture of openness and curiosity. It is no mistake that caregivers from different cultural perspectives and different denominational and religious traditions converge on this point. Caring for children is a big and meaningful job. Many of us feel pressure to get it right, maybe without a clear conception of what right would even look like. In this context, we might struggle to loosen the reigns and get curious about our kids' thoughts and feelings without trying to control or mold their responses. We invite you to do it anyway. We hope the reflections included provide evidence supporting the fruitfulness of this approach.

Think about this volume as a pick-your-own-adventure book. While you are welcome to move through in a linear fashion, there is no need to. These reflections cover the gamut of your parenting or caregiving life. Some days, you may need some insight into a particular experience. Then, you can use the table of contents to guide you. On other days, you may just be wondering (or wandering) and need to hear from another caregiver. Open the book up and see where it takes you. We hope this book will end up being tattered, earmarked, and well-used, and it will meet you at many points in your caregiving journey.

Each reflection is organized in a Read-Think-Pray-Act format. We begin with a story, and the author shares their reflections on what that story means. Then, you are offered a prayer and an action to take moving forward. Despite the busyness and frenzy you may sometimes find in your life, we invite you to stop and take a few breaths before encountering each reflection. Give yourself a moment to center and be present to take in the lessons offered. Actually pray the prayer, aloud or silently, as you invite God to energize and anoint your caregiving. Commit to trying your version of the actions suggested in the reflections. Please note that the actions are an invitation rather than a prescription. You may find yourself adjusting to fit your cultural, social, or practical reality. In essence, do what works for you!

In compiling this volume, we gathered reflections that cover a wide range of caregiving experiences. Despite the great diversity of the experiences and backgrounds of our contributors, you will find several predominant themes that show up across reflections. Several authors hone in on the power of rituals, or the things we do regularly that set up expectations in our families and send strong messages about who we are and who God is. These reflections range from bedtime blessings to the family spiritual practices in which we engage to the way we approach engagement in faith communities and other communities of support.

Other authors invite us to consider the vastness of children's sensory experiences and how these can be used to build relationships and teach. From songs to children's observations of the visual environment to messy sensory experiences, these authors remind us that everything is a learning opportunity.

Some authors invite us into the power of storytelling. Their reflections provide poignant perspectives on stories as a pathway for autonomy, critical thinking, and connection with the Divine. They also recognize that, in addition to a more informal process, stories can be used explicitly by caregivers as a tool for connection and reflection.

Some authors provide tools for tackling difficult conversations about death, sin, suffering, and salvation. These authors push us to lean into uncertainty and to recognize that children's big questions deserve our attention and time, even when (especially when) we do not have the answers. Many note specifically how important it is to acknowledge the big emotions that are inherent in the human experience.

Yet more reflections nudge caregivers to loosen up and let children be. Several authors reflect on times when children did not behave as the adults hoped they should and the good that came out of it. They name caregiving as a privilege, and we can honor that by adjusting our expectations or behaviors that allow us to be curious with the children we love.

Finally, we offer a word about *faith*. Faith and faithfulness come in many forms. The reflections in this resource draw up a variety of understandings about faith and faithfulness through the lens of the authors who share them. Some of these understandings will align with your own. Some will challenge your traditions and perceptions, and that is okay. Use these reflections as an opportunity to lean in and get curious about the insights available to you in forms of faith and faithfulness that seem different from your own as well as those that feel familiar.

One more thing—if you find this resource helpful, you may want to share it with other parents and caregivers. We encourage you to do so! And if you would like to dig deeper into the questions and issues raised in this book, you might be interested in its companion volume filled with accessible scholarship to equip you to become more intentional in raising faithful kids. Maybe you will read the companion resource with a group of other parents and caregivers as you share the journey of raising faithful kids together.

Notes

1. Christian Smith and Amy Adamczyk, *Handing Down the Faith: How Parents Pass Their Religion on to the Next Generation* (New York: Oxford University Press, 2021), 1–2.

2. The Lilly Endowment, Inc., the largest funder of theological education in the US, recently awarded grants to seventy-seven organizations for up to $1.25 million each that build on this research to resource parents and caregivers.

Section I
The Power of Ritual

Rituals can be some of the most powerful experiences of childhood. Whether these are formal traditions and practices or not, they leave a powerful imprint on children. The authors in this section invite you to think about the power associated with rituals and traditions. These repetitive practices have the power to transmit implicit and explicit messages about what your family thinks and believes. As you read the reflections in this section, consider whether your practices and traditions are sharing what you hope to share.

1

Faith that Is More *Caught* than Taught...

JENNA WILLIAMS

Read

As a mom of three young boys, life is busy. The list of stuff that keeps us busy and my mind twirling is endless: school, practices, playdates, carpools, homework, and so much more. And then there are the basic daily tasks of ensuring the kids (and myself) have healthy meals, clean clothes, and an organized house so they can find their stuff on the way out to an activity. I admit religion and the religious education of my children sometimes take a back seat to all the other things.

I grew up Catholic, and my husband grew up in a very conservative Lutheran church. My husband's experience in the church of his youth turned him away from church and religion. We both agree religious education is an important part of our children's upbringing, but most of the decision-making in this area falls on me.

Growing up, I went through phases of being more involved in church than others, but I felt faith was a constant. I found myself using my faith and belief in God to help me accept and explain things I may not have yet had the developmental capacity to comprehend. As an adult, I may not approach difficult situations with the same verbiage as I did as a child, but I still find myself using the same strategies of finding the positive or having faith in difficult situations. Reflecting on the role I want religion and faith to play in my children's upbringing, the situations when I turn to faith become the focal point of the faith modeling I hope to do with my children. Like so many, we turn to faith and religion during difficult times. Something as simple as a disappointment of not getting a good grade despite studying hard or something more tragic, such as a death in the family, can provide opportunities for dialogue about faith. As a child, my grounding in faith helped me look at such situations calmly and to work through my complex feelings. Those strategies and skills of faith and religion helped me develop and have carried over into how I approach difficult situations as an adult.

Although we are not weekly churchgoers or heavily involved in church, I think it is important my children understand religion and its role in their lives, especially when difficult or complex situations arise, such as those they may not be developmentally ready to understand.

Think

At times, I feel alone in this journey of forming faith with my children, wondering if I am doing it right. Then I remind myself that, like so much in parenting, there is no right or wrong answer but simply different paths people choose to take, each yielding different outcomes. My ultimate goal as a parent is to raise children who are kind and respectful, and help make the world a better place. As I model my faith with them, I hope they are growing to see faith as a tool to equip them to live out those values.

Pray

God, help me raise my children to reflect the best of what you created humanity to be: kind and respectful, helping to make the world a better place, knowing that your grace wraps us all in your love. Amen.

Act

Whether you feel like you are winning at parenting/caregiving today or simply trying to survive, breathe in God's grace and exhale the guilt. God loves you and the children in your life more than you know. Keep doing your best, trusting that God's grace is enough.

2

Blessing Our Children

THOMAS RAWLS

Read

When our three kids were little, we felt that it was important to establish a pattern of prayer for them. So, we did the things we experienced growing up in Christian families: we blessed the food before dinner, and we prayed with them before bed. I must admit, I hit a point where those bedtime prayers became more difficult to maintain, especially when the kids were tired and fussy. Sometimes I was tired and fussy. Prayer time began to feel forced, but I did not want to give the practice up entirely. One night, I simply did not have it in me to try to make them say a prayer. Instead, I placed my hands on their heads and said a short blessing: "God bless you and keep you, and give you rest." The effect was remarkable. Instead of something forced, the blessing offered a moment of calm and peace before sleep. I hope this moment communicated both my love for them as their father and God's constant presence and care for them. Years have passed, but the nightly blessings continue. Two of our kids are teenagers, and the third will be all too soon, but the three still allow me to give them a hug or place my hands on their heads while I ask God to bless them.

Think

The process of forming faith in our families includes everything we say and do. It involves the example we set for our children as well as the lessons we explicitly try to teach them. But the things that have the biggest and most lasting impact are the things we do and say repeatedly. The repetition communicates the importance and helps those things to stick. Think of the family stories that are told and retold at every gathering. They create a shared sense of identity (who we are as a family) and values (what it means to be a Rawls, for example). In the same way, consistency is the most important aspect of any faith practice. A small thing done repeatedly will have a greater impact than a big thing done once.

Pray

Loving God, whose constant presence both comforts and challenges us, we ask you to give us grace to speak and act consistently, that we may model a faith that is truly a blessing for our children, and give us grace for the times we fall short. Amen.

Act

Say a word of blessing to the children in your care today. Every family is different; decide on a time and place that makes sense to you. Find or write something that expresses the blessing you want to share: it may be something from Scripture, but it could also come from a favorite song or poem. Keep it short and simple, and do not worry if it feels awkward.

3

Music in the Air

EMILY BRYANT

Read

Four of us live in a small one-story house: my husband, our two elementary-aged children, and me. In the middle of this house is a stereo that my husband bought with his savings when he was a teenager, over twenty years ago. The stereo does not have many features, but that is okay. Its only job these days is to remain tuned to the local Christian radio station. We keep it on almost 24/7. Like most things that are so readily available to us (such as running water, oxygen, or God's love), we alternatively take it for granted or feel grateful and appreciative for it. Sometimes, it is background music, barely noticeable and taking a backseat to whatever else is happening in the room. Other times, we find ourselves singing along to the songs, looking up the music videos on YouTube, and talking about the spiritual themes in the lyrics together. We groan at the corny jokes that the DJs tell, feel impatient at the seemingly endless pledge drives, or complain about how the station seems to only play five songs on repeat. This station has given our family a common spiritual ground. Last year, we drove an hour to watch a favorite band in concert together. Sometimes, my son will write down the lyrics to a favorite song and post it by his bed. He has shared his favorite Christian music videos with his school friend. His friend's dad jokes that it has messed up his finely-tuned You-Tube algorithm.

Think

There are many practical ways to develop a rich spiritual life in children. In the busyness of our lives, my husband and I do not have a great track record of having family devotional time or reading Scripture together. Frankly, I am unsure that I have a great track record with having a good attitude toward God all the time. The radio has been, quite literally, a God send. It is consistent when we cannot be. The music tenderly normalizes and validates the ups and downs of the Christian life. It often helps lift moods of shame, embarrassment, or sadness that flit in and out of our days. Our humble little stereo continues to share hopeful Good News. The local radio station DJs continue sharing their corny jokes and earnest prayers for the community. The station is sponsored in part by listeners, who share their testimonies of how God has met them in times of trouble. I thank God that these good things are in the air in our house. How can you make the air good in your home?

Pray

Lord, thank you for the musicians, radio DJs, and all the others in the community who work to fill the radio waves with the Good News. We pray that the songs of faithfulness will work their way into the hearts of our children so that when they are feeling scared or lonely in the world, they will remember the songs and be encouraged by the love of God.

Act

Consider leaving a Christian radio station on in your house or car. Try it for a month and see what happens.

4

A Parent's Role

CARMICHAEL D. CRUTCHFIELD

Read

When our son was five years old, he was preparing to sing in the children's choir at a worship service. Then, I overheard one of the directors of the choir ask him, "Where did you learn to sing so well?"

He quickly responded, "Ask my daddy; he knows everything."

At a parent-teacher meeting, our daughter's first-grade teacher told us our child had an unfair advantage. She said, "Each time your daughter is given a test, she bows her head and tells me she is praying."

I reflect now on these two early childhood experiences of our children in light of our son's service as a military chaplain and our daughter's recent ordination and employment with a foster care agency. These memories have been a source of great thought about the role of parents in the early years of their children. On the one hand, parents provide a feeling of security that embodies a sense of direction and wisdom that is perfect—at least in the mind of a little five-year-old who believes his daddy knows everything. But my thoughts go deeper as I reflect upon the dependence children have on their parents or caregivers.

My son's words, "ask my daddy. . . ." reflect confidence in a parent to do and say the right thing all the time. His words exude confidence in the parent to always act with wisdom. This reflection causes me to think about how my parents and relatives would not allow the children to be present during some conversations that they called "adult." As I became an adult, it became obvious to me that those adults were not perfect, but they were certain that the children should not hear some of the conversations that reflected their imperfections.

Now, I turn to what our daughter's first-grade teacher told us as her parents. At the time, I was not a preacher, so I wondered what caused our daughter to believe prayer was in order prior to taking a test. Her mother and I did not teach her explicitly to pray under those circumstances. However, she would have heard us pray at home and sometimes at church.

But the more I reflect on the words of our daughter's first-grade teacher, the more I am convinced it had much to do with a "village" that was amplified in a small church Sunday school, where she had attended her first six years of life. As I reflect further and think about this experience, she and her brother were always with us in church for prayer meetings, Bible study, and church meetings. In all these places, people prayed. She was exposed to prayer in her young life.

Think

So, this reflection causes me to think deeply about the responsibilities parents have concerning the spiritual nurture of their children. The word that comes to mind is exposure. It is not so much about lectures or reading the Bible, but about exposing our children to those things that might engender a relationship with God. At the same time, parents have the responsibility to embody spirituality. Each generation, person, family, or group might experience this differently. For example, bedtime prayer was a staple for me growing up, but it was not for my children.

The bottom line of these two stories is that children look up to their parents and caregivers. Parents and caregivers have the responsibility of caring for their children in a way that children feel secure to the point of believing there is no limit to a parent's care. This care includes spiritual aspects that lead to a relationship with God.

Pray

Lord, help me to embody a wholeness that gives my children confidence and emboldens them throughout life.

Act

Ask children to put together a collage of pictures that represent their family. Parents and caregivers will need to assist with finding pictures, identify/naming persons, and more.

5

Learning to Pray from a Kneeling Father

EVELYN L. PARKER

Read

*"I watched you many a night as you kneeled
by your bed,
eyes closed and rubbing your head while con-
versing with Jesus."*

These words are an excerpt from the tribute that my nephew, André M. "Sport" Parker, wrote in his tribute to my father, Jesse "Poe" Parker, after he died. The poem was titled "For What It's Worth," written for the program of my dad's funeral, Friday, May 9, 2008. I never asked André why he titled the poem this way. From reading the entire tribute, I guess it was because he never told my dad how much he loved, admired, and emulated him. André was in Atlanta when my dad made his transition. I knew, for André, that not being able to talk to his granddad during the final moments of his granddad's life was painful. So, "For What It's Worth" was written for all who would read the funeral program and gave witness to Sport's love for Poe.

As I read the poem fifteen years later, I realized that my dad formed André's Christian beliefs and practices in several ways, including the spiritual practice of prayer. My dad taught André, me, and all those who loved him how to pray. He modeled prayer in private, kneeling at his bedside, his tall six-foot three-inch frame curved around the edge of his bed, rubbing his head, talking softly in conversation with God. I remember standing behind him, listening to my dad pray. Sometimes the words were audible, filled with passion, a petition to God of some sort. Then, there were his public prayers—in local churches, Sunday school, church conferences, and even while attending national meetings of the Christian Methodist Episcopal Church. He would bend his long legs to pray at his pew. Most often, he would stand straight with his head bowed and eyes closed while talking to God on behalf of the congregation. Both private and public prayers had certain postures and positions of the body while my dad prayed.

Not only did my dad teach us postures for praying, but he also taught us what to pray for—the content of prayer. He did not have a formula, but somehow, he would always offer words of thanks, intercessions on behalf of family and friends, prayers for members of the congregation—the sick, the bereaved, the homeless, the unemployed, the incarcerated—and petitions to God. My dad always insisted that we pray together, holding hands before traveling. If we were rushing and did not follow the travel prayer ritual, he would pray at the steering wheel, with his eyes wide open, that God would keep us safe from car accidents and any other dangers, "seen and unseen." I loved his insistence, although I never admitted it, to hold my hand and pray before I traveled back to college by bus from Mississippi to Tennessee, or drove back to work in Galveston, Texas, in my small gray Chevrolet Chevette, or even drove back to seminary in Dallas, Texas, many years later. Although in my immature resistance, I would think, "It doesn't take all that." Now, I realize how my dad's travel prayers gave me confidence that God was with me as I drove four hundred or more miles, sometimes in thunderstorms and on icy highways. Travel prayers, all sorts of public and private prayers were how we learned to pray from my dad.

Think

Children learn how to pray best when they see adults whom they love praying. The posture for praying or the content of the prayers is not important. The primary requirement is that the love of God flows as does the love of the child.

Pray

Loving God, teach us to pray as we ought with love that flows from you to those we love—our children, our friends, our family, our congregation, all people of every nation, and all creation. Lord Jesus, teach us to pray like you taught your disciples.

Holy Spirit, intercede for us with utterances that only you can understand.

Act

Teach the children that you love how to pray. The Lord's Prayer is the best starting point.

6

Serving Children More than Food

DIANE JANSSEN HEMMEN

Read

My starting point regarding the basic care of children has always been food. Maybe it was the hovering, passionate lactation nurse's multiple "supportive" visits beginning in the hospital on the eve of my first delivery. My concern that the children be well nourished and not hungry has been reflexive (nearly archetypal) since each cord was cut. And it seemed natural to me that this concern for nourishment would extend to exposing my children to larger issues of food insecurity.

This concern wove its way into the raising of our children early in their lives. During their late preschool and kindergarten years, they were adding cookies to the trays that were served at the monthly shelter meals. In elementary school, they were adding international awareness as part of a shippable food packing event with the nonprofit "Feed My Starving Children" in which our wider family participated. Middle and high school years brought some awareness of food deserts, as drives to athletic events and the high school itself included viewing the shuttered grocery store in the downtown area, as well as a week abroad in Costa Rica during which they mostly ate rice, beans, and gray water.

None of that exposure or teaching hung together until we put words to it, until we spoke to the children succinctly about why we were continuing to poke a finger in the damaged dike or pay attention to which candidates said they would work to bring accessible food back to the heart of the city. In their early years, our teaching sounded like, "Each day is a gift from God," or singing the clapping song, "We love (clap, clap) because God first loved us." Gradually, the children grew into young adults who came to their own realizations of the complexities of basic needs being met in overwhelming circumstances, but the habit of restating with the greatest possible simplicity the "why" of what we were doing as a response to God's grace in our lives has been and remains an essential shared practice of faith.

Think

It is not uncommon for those with food and other necessities in life to give very little thought to those facing food scarcity. Exposing our children to the world of hunger can be done in simple ways, such as involving them with opportunities to serve food banks and other entities that address food scarcity. It could even be a family project.

Pray

Gracious God, when problems seem larger than our hearts can hold and beyond us, keep us hopeful that they are not bigger than you. Grant us courageous kindness on this day; help us notice the needs around us and do one thing for someone else.

Act

Invite the family to share things they like doing for others—making family dinner, helping with errands, foot rubs, cheering at the track meet—and calendar opportunities in the next two weeks to do those things together. At least bi-monthly, repeat these enjoyments of using God's gifts to us in ways that bless others.

7

Reflections on Parenting from a Religious/Christian Educator

MARY A. LOVE

Read

I have had numerous opportunities to observe parental engagement with the younger generation promoting faith formation. Is there such a thing as a model parent or caregiver? The Smiths in my church impress me as a model of parenthood. Although I am not a parent, this family is one example of parents making a difference in the faith development of the younger generation. Over time, I have seen this family at home and in public spaces, including the church.

The Smiths are very intentional in their spiritual practices as parents. I once asked them about their attribute regarding their children's involvement in the life of the church. They spoke about some rituals in their home. One such ritual is prayer and the children's involvement in the prayer time. This leads to reading the Bible aloud, talking about the biblical accounts, and singing hymns or some popular gospel music.

The Smiths are the epitome of consistency. Like all adults, life presents many challenges regarding the availability of time. However, the Smiths maneuver in such a way that the children do not suffer because of their busyness. Their rituals of reading the Scripture, prayer at bedtime, and other designated times seem to be priorities.

During the height of the COVID-19 crisis, the consistency continued when virtual church became the norm for worship and ministry with the younger generation was all but forsaken. The Smiths encouraged their local church to provide worship and study in a way that kept the younger generation involved. To this end, the Smiths bought the necessary software so the family could play games at home with meaning. I do not know the names of the games, but they were things that the entire family enjoyed. Beyond this, the Smiths were leaders in helping the church to use online games like Kahoot! to engage all ages.

Think

Parents must be intentional with the younger generation by engaging in faith practices with them. Provide opportunities for the younger generation to practice reverence for God. They can also engage in spiritual practices such as prayer, reading the Bible, and conversation as ways to assist in their faith formation.

Pray

O God, help me to draw near to you and to be a good role model. Help me to think before I act and to look beyond actions to consequences of the actions. Enable me to practice love in all situations and actions. Amen.

Act

Take a walk with the young ones and be intentional in noting various things (birds, flowers, trees, butterflies, animals, clouds) that are a part of God's creation. Use examples from science lessons at school and provide faith connections. Engage them in examining what they see on the various media outlets. Discuss the consequences of certain behaviors and share biblical references to build faith connections. Help the younger generation to value life and understand the consequences of violent behavior. Develop rituals and practices that have faith connections. For example, as members of the younger generation reach certain milestones, be intentional in giving praise and giving God thanks. Point out divine activity (modern-day miracles) in the lives of people. Engage with other parents to share meaningful practices that are useful. Develop a parent support group.

8

Building Relationships

KEOSHA BRANCH

Read

Religion has always been a part of my life. I grew up in a very religious family. We went to church every Sunday, Bible study youth group on Wednesdays, and prayer service on Fridays. If the doors to the church were open, we were there. I knew the Word and all the Bible stories, and I could quote Scripture from a young age. I loved attending church, but I had a love/hate relationship with religion. I was very devout, mainly because I feared going to hell. I strived to follow all the rules—especially the dos and don'ts! I was driven by fear and guilt. It was exhausting. It was not until my college years that I grew and developed a *relationship* with Jesus Christ. I learned the difference between religion and relationship, and my spirituality flourished.

As a parent, it was imperative that I taught my children to develop a relationship with God from an early age. I did not want to preach religion to them. I wanted to demonstrate how to build and maintain a relationship with God. I did not want a fear of hell to drive them to obedience. I wanted their obedience to flow out of love and devotion to God. My husband and I were intentional about having our children see and hear us pray, read the Word, and spend time in worship. We made prayer a part of their daily lives and taught them how to pray. We read the Bible with them and taught them how to memorize Scripture. We taught them the power of praise and how our worship connects us to God. We did this as a family in our home in addition to attending church and getting them involved in the children's ministry at church.

Think

Honestly, the pandemic was pivotal in helping my children foster a relationship with God. It was an uncertain time for everybody, me included. I was worried, and openly talked about my worries in an age-appropriate way with my children as I explained why they could not go to school anymore and why we weren't going to church or other activities. We had many conversations about God's love for us, protection over us, and power to heal us. We discussed how we could talk to God whenever we wanted to about anything we had on our minds. They saw my husband and I spend time praying and reading the Bible, and they began to mirror these behaviors over time. My hope is that this early exposure will be a foundation that they are able to carry with them throughout the rest of their lives.

Pray

Lord, thank you for blessing me with my children. Please help me to demonstrate to them how to build a relationship with you based on love and devotion. Reveal to me how to best foster and encourage them to develop their own personal relationship with you. In Jesus' name. Amen.

Act

Begin a weekly family Bible study on the topic of prayer. Teach your children to pray using the Lord's Prayer as a model.

9

It Takes a Faith Community

WILLA M. ROSS

Read

At the age of eight years old, my daughter was asked by the pastor to read the weekly church announcements. She was a very curious child who loved to read and interact with others. The church we attended had a vibrant and active children's ministry. The pastor was intentional about involving children in worship. Almost every Sunday following church service, my daughter asked questions about different service components. She was a member of the children's choir and loved to sing songs about Jesus. One day, I heard my daughter teaching the song "Jesus Loves Me" to one of her younger cousins and explaining to her why Jesus loved her. I also recall her reading the Sunday school lesson to a group of her cousins on another occasion. At other times, she and her older brother and younger sister sang gospel songs during our travels in the car.

The same pastor who asked my daughter to read the announcements mentored my son. My children were fortunate to be a part of a church family that intentionally nurtured children in the faith. All three of them were given the opportunity to use their talents and gifts to actively participate in the life of the church. They learned who God was and how God called them to love and serve others. Their faith journey began within a congregation where children were cherished and were a part of the body of Christ.

Think

When my children and I united with the above congregation, I was a single young adult parent. Although they knew who Jesus was, they knew very little about the importance of being involved in the life of the church. The pastor and members, along with their grandmother, were instrumental in teaching them about faith. Now that they are all mature adults with families of their own, they recognize the importance and impact of the body of Christ sharing in the faith formation not only of their children but all children.

Pray

Faithful and nurturing God, instill in parents and caregivers a passion to engage and actively participate in ways that give children the curiosity to explore the church and come to know that Jesus loves them.

Act

Children desire to be accepted and included. Take time to reach out to a child and ask them what the church means to them. Invite them to participate in worship or some other practice of the church. Engage in conversation with their parents and/or caregivers about encouraging them.

10

Celebrating Children: Inspiring Congregational Vitality

MARY H. YOUNG

Read

I once pastored a church that sat in the heart of an urban community, where it had been for ninety-eight years. During its impressive heyday, worshipers needed to arrive almost an hour early to get a good seat. All age groups were present in the vibrant worshiping faith community. Children participated in the service and sang in the children's choir. However, by its ninety-eighth year, the congregation had become very different. It was time for a new vision and a fresh beginning that could outshine those relished former years. What we did not know was that God would use children from our community as the catalysts for breathing new life into the church.

Couched in a challenging and stressed urban context where crime, poverty, and other social concerns abounded, our church needed a good shot in the arm. Families with children had grown up in the church throughout the years, but they grew up. The grown children moved on and out, leaving noticeable gaps in the church's life-cycle groups. But this ninety-eighth year, through the evangelistic efforts of our young adults, God blessed us with an influx of children from our community. They easily filled three to four pews in the congregation and their ages ranged from about five to twelve years old. The presence of the children brought new vitality into the congregation and challenged us to develop intentional, relevant, and creative discipleship ministries for them.

As a congregation, we became surrogate parents for the children God entrusted to our care. Ironically, though many never attended church on a regular basis, they had an almost insatiable desire to learn, grow, and be involved. The children loved hugs, smiles, and affirmative words. As their pastor, I gave of those things generously each Sunday when they ran to me after the benediction. But there were many other caregiving acts shared between our congregation and the children. One specific incident occurred during a Sunday morning worship experience when a ten-year-old child led worship for youth day. The child exhibited amazing bravery and did so well with practicing the task prior to the service. But a few minutes into the role, he had trouble reading through the items on the printed bulletin and showed noticeable signs of fear and embarrassment. At that time, one of our ministerial associates walked up to the podium where the child stood and placed his arm around him. The ministerial associate spoke calmly and affirmatively, encouraging the child to take his time and assuring him that he could do it. When the task was completed, the congregation gave a rousing applause and shouts of "Amen." With a contagious smile on his face and a vivacious pep in his steps, the child returned to his seat in confidence and calmness.

Think

Believing that intentional religious activity is important for early childhood spiritual formation, our congregation's embracing the gift of children was connected to John Westerhoff's *experienced faith* stage of human development. Westerhoff believes that such initial encounters, grounded in the child's vivid and developing imagination, are foundational for further faith development.[1] For both the preschool and elementary-age children in our church, it was important that through our practices of acceptance and belonging, they would come to know the love of God and others. Our church embraced the gift of young people and became revitalized and inspired by the work in our community. Their presence was a blessing in disguise.

Pray

Gracious Lord, grant that we might welcome the gift of children in our midst and prepare us to both bless and be a blessing to them as we guide the way to your feet.

Act

As a parent, caregiver, or spiritual guide to children, take the time and exercise the patience to let a child lead the way. For instance, in the case of participation in worship, encourage them through their mistakes, affirm them amid their doubts, and be open to the ways God will use them to inspire your own faith.

Note

1. John Westerhoff, *Will Our Children Have Faith?* (Toronto: Anglican Book Centre, 2000), 89ff.

11

The Role of the Church in Caregiving

WILLA M. ROSS

Read

As a single mother of three now adult children, I am keenly aware of the role the church plays in forming and shaping the lives of young people. Regardless of the biological make up of the family, the support and care provided by a faith community can significantly impact the life of a child.

While serving as a pastor in Tennessee, I was blessed to lead a church where the members took their responsibility to nurture the youth of the congregation seriously. Three of the youth in that congregation were young girls from single-parent homes. Although they often attended church with their grandmother, they had low self-esteem and resented the fact that their mothers were raising them alone. They also felt unaccepted by their peers and unloved by family members.

Upon developing a relationship with these three young girls, we discerned their need for guidance and trust from those who claimed to care for them. We recognized their need for safe spaces where their stories could be heard and not judged. They needed caregivers and mentors who were open to listening not only to their stories but also to their angst and rage as well. They felt an overall need to belong and to be loved.

Over a four-year period, the lives of these three young girls were transformed. Their self-esteem blossomed as they began the process of becoming their authentic selves. The impact of the care and support provided by the body of Christ brought about a change in the way they viewed their family, the church, and the larger community. They developed a sense of purpose along with a desire to strive to be better and do better. The church recognized the significant impact they had in this transformation.

Think

How can faith communities and leaders contribute to the healthy emotional and spiritual well-being of all children? What are some of the ways faith communities can nurture the children in their care?

Pray

Loving and caring God, fill us with the love needed to be faithful mentors and caregivers who you call to nurture this generation of children.

Act

Be intentional in listening to children. Make eye contact, give them your undivided attention, and let them know that you hear what they are telling you.

Section II
Sensory Experiences

Any review of developmental theories of childhood will tell you how primary sensory experiences are during childhood. As we age, we tend to gravitate more toward our thinking and away from our embodied experiences. These authors encourage you to recognize the importance of all the senses in the faith lives of children.

12

Let's Get Messy

DURECIA D. MOORER

Read

On one particular Sunday, I gathered a sack of oranges and a huge bowl of water, eagerly anticipating the arrival of a diverse group of energized children for the children's church session I was leading at my church.

As they entered the room and spotted the bowl of water, curiosity sparked a myriad of questions about what Minister D had in store for the day. After a quick snack, we delved into our lesson. Each child received an orange with a simple instruction to drop their oranges into the water—which, of course, they did with as much force as they could muster. The result was a cascade of oranges plunging into the water, creating playful splashes all around. To the children's amazement, these seemingly ordinary oranges possessed the extraordinary ability to float! The mystery behind this phenomenon awaited revelation.

Next, I guided them to retrieve their oranges from the water and then peel them. Soon, a chorus of squeals, requests for assistance, sticky fingers, and impatience to be the first to unveil their oranges filled the air. With reassurance that no one would be left struggling, every orange was successfully peeled.

With gleeful anticipation of their reaction, I said, "On my ready, drop your oranges into the water!" Astonishment echoed through the room as the oranges descended into the water and settled at the bowl's bottom. "Oh, my goodness, the orange sank!" and "How did that happen?" rang out from excited voices.

Think

We all need opportunities to tangibly experience lessons through all five senses. Water splashing everywhere, sticky fingers, boisterous reactions—all become holy tools for encountering God. Faith is best shared with our children by engaging their innate ability to be inquisitive, creative, and imaginative learners.

Pray

God, you are *Creator*, and therefore I possess *creativity* that allows me to get messy as one *created* in your image! Help me step outside of the box and my comfort zone to help our children experience you in a unique way. Amen.

Act

Consider something in your surroundings that could be used to share faith through some or all the senses. Use this as a tool to help children look, listen, feel, taste, and smell together as we live our faith.

13

A Grown-up Song

TAMAR WASOIAN

Read

I loved our lunchtime with the four-year-old class at daycare. That was the time for us to sit down and talk. Between serving the food and cleaning up, I made sure the children had my attention. We talked about the morning, food, or anything they had on their mind. On one of those days, one little boy started humming and singing. He knew we did not sing during lunch, but he kept singing and looking at me from the corner of his eye. My first reaction was to remind him of the "no singing" rule but stopped myself from it. He was trying to communicate something with me. I asked, "Where did you learn this song?" There was something different about this song. It was not any of the children's upbeat ones. It was what we at the church would call a "grown-up song." He smiled, affirming that I asked the right question. He told me that he had learned the song at the temple.

Soon the other children started humming "grown-up songs" that they knew. They then shared where they learned the songs.

Think

Often, music choices are made for children by adults. This incident helped me see that I might be wrong in my assumptions about what kind of musical experiences children need. Upbeat and simple rhythms are catchy and fun, but why limit children's music choices? Singing a children's song or hymn during worship often signals dismissing the children off to their program. Could it be possible that the children are communicating that they like singing the grown-ups songs because they can sing them with the grown-up's? Being together with the community is what is valued here, and singing hymns plays a significant part in worship. Maybe it is about being part of the community and what the community does together during worship where the value truly lies.

Pray

Heavenly Parent, teach us to respect our
    children.
Help us see your creative image in them.
Help us nurture them in your wisdom and
    love.

Act

Next time you attend the church service online or in person, make sure to have the hymnal on hand and help your child follow the printed words and the music notes. You will be surprised at how engaged and excited they would be. The church that sings together, grows together.

14

Introducing the Holy Spirit as the True and Good Shepherd

CHARIS GOODMAN

Read

When I meet new groups of children, I teach them a song about the fruits of the Spirit, which allows vocabulary to be stored in their minds and hearts immediately. Later, we inevitably reach a point where we encounter feelings or behaviors that feel bigger than us. On the board, I write "God" and have the children name the fruits of the Spirit, which I connect around it like sun rays or flower petals. Then, I invite the class to help me figure out a hard, big, challenging feeling or behavior, and I write it on the board and draw a line to connect it with the fruit that can be used to manage it. Students are then able to connect their feelings and behavior needs to a provision of the Holy Spirit they are familiar with from the song. Long-term memories are created. For their sadness, there is joy, gentleness, and peace. For their desire to lash out in anger, there is self-control and love. As weeks go by, students come to find that they can ask God directly for what they need, being in tune with their body (similar to a mindfulness body scan), aware of their emotions and their effects on others, which develops self-regulation skills and empathy. Most importantly, they can reorient their perspectives to seek God's truth for guidance as the core concept of problem-solving and provision-seeking. That is training they can carry throughout their lives.

Think

In the Bible, we learn to train children in the ways that they should go so that when they are old, they will not turn from them. Sometimes we are not able to live up to that call—we all have limitations. We plan good activities, methods, and strategies, but ultimately, children emulate the authorities they have regular exposure to. As careful and curating as we can be, we will never be or find perfect human role models. We need to shift who we see as the authority.

As I watch generation upon generation of my elders, peers, and former students develop, I become increasingly disenchanted with a sort of watch me/hero complex paradigm that can easily sneak into any role where one feels they have something—wisdom, experience, method, innovation, information, skill—to pass down to, to pour into, to set upon those who come behind. My approach to spiritual formation in children was transformed by the concept of coming alongside children as siblings in Christ with a fundamental adjustment to invite the Holy Spirit to be the true teacher and authority. This allows grace for our humanness and the capacity for children to grow and develop beyond our limitations.

Pray

Lord, as we seek to shepherd children well, help us to look to you as the true and Good Shepherd of us all. May you grant us the humility and continual awareness to walk in paths of righteousness alongside our younger brothers and sisters, inviting the fruits of your Holy Spirit to grow and ripen in our daily walks with you.

Act

Make a practice of helping children identify and recognize the challenges in their lives and have conversations about how God can help us in our moments of challenge.

15

The Sounds and Shape of Love

RACHEL PIERCE

Read

"Sing my song, Mama." These are the words that come from my almost five-year-old each night after we read a book. As a professional singer, it was natural that I would sing lullabies to my children during our bedtime routine each night. Over the last five years of singing to my children, I have learned that the practice of daily rituals and reminders of love are shaping me as much as I pray and believe they are shaping them.

As a music student at Radford University, I learned "The Lord Bless You and Keep You" by Peter C. Lutkin/arr. by Lloyd Larson. A beautiful four-part arrangement that is written from The Aaronic Blessing that Aaron and his sons were to speak over the people of Israel, recorded in the book of Numbers. The lyrics read, "The Lord bless you and keep you; The Lord make his face shine on you and be gracious to you; The Lord turn his face toward you and give you peace." These words resonated with me deeply, and the sound of our voices in the choir was holy. Each time I sang this song in college, there was a presence that even some who did not have a faith practice would describe as sacred. It stuck with me and years later, I watched a dear friend pray these words over his children before bed each night. One time, when leaving their home in Colorado and getting back on a plane headed to Virginia, he and his wife prayed this prayer over me. It was so significant that I knew when I had children of my own, I would sing/speak these words over them regularly. So, I did.

When my firstborn came, I sang these words to her. Then the pandemic came. An artist named Kari Jobe released a version of "The Blessing" with a different tune and added lyrics. She sang, "May His favor be upon you, and a thousand generations, and your family and your children, and their children, and their children; May His presence go before you, and behind you, and beside you, all around you, and within you; He is with you, he is with you . . . Amen, amen, amen; Amen, amen, amen." I remember hearing it for the first time and weeping. I was asking myself questions like, "How are we going to get through this? How will this pandemic impact our family? My work? Her development?" And then, I began to sing. I sang this blessing over and over and over. I wanted her to hear it—I needed to hear it—and it became our anthem. We sang it while taking walks, playing in the yard, and, of course, each night before bed. Now, as an almost five-year-old, when she says, "Sing my song, Mama," she means, start with "May His presence" and finish with the traditional Lloyd Larson arrangement. It makes my heart smile.

Think

On the nights when I am exhausted from working and parenting, the words are just as much for me as they are for her, and even when I am frustrated, these words soften my heart and my spirit and remind me of these ancient texts that are sacred markers for our lives and our hearts.

Pray

"The Lord bless you and keep you;
The Lord make his face shine on you and be
gracious to you;
The Lord turn his face toward you and give
you peace." —Numbers 6:25-26 NIV

Act

Consider a simple blessing or prayer you can share with the children in your life as a ritual and a reminder of the divine presence and of your love for them. Let it become your special sacred time together when you sing your song or share words that have (or will have) special significance for you and your family.

16

Spring Break Rituals

BARBARA ANNETTE FEARS

Read

From mid-elementary through middle school, my nephew spent spring breaks with me in Chicago, Illinois. Over these years, we had established rituals from which we never deviated. From the airport, we went to Olive Garden for his favorite meal, to the grocery store for his favorite foods, to Blockbuster to rent whatever movies he chose to watch for the week. Each day, we had a meal (e.g., breakfast, lunch, or dinner) at a restaurant and an activity (e.g., movie, zoo, museum, aquarium, ballet, theater, cruise, Art Institute, Sears Tower, Trinity United Church of Christ, and seminary class) in the city.

My nephew started these daily adventures with enthusiasm (e.g., zoo, movie), disinterest (e.g., Art Institute), and suspicion (e.g., Alvin Ailey Ballet). At each event, he found something that captured his attention (even the ballet), thereby providing opportunities for in-depth reflection on an array of topics, including God, sacred presence, and his own Christian faith formation. We discussed spiritual messages conveyed in *The Lion King*, and subtle but dangerous messaging in music. Sometimes, he initiated a spiritual formation discussion with a question about something that intrigued him. Other times, I initiated these discussions by asking what he perceived about sacred presence in the acting, art, dance, music, and sermon. Our ritual was to conclude these discussions with how he too was a self-expression of the *imago Dei.*

Think

These ordinary interactions with my nephew reflect teaching-learning exchanges proffered by John Dewey who believed education is both active and interactive and involves the social world of the child and of the community.[1] These exchanges also reflect the theories of Lev Vygotsky who emphasized play in children's learning and stretching children's knowledge via the zone of proximal development, the distance between the actual development level as determined by independent problem-solving and the level of potential development under adult guidance or in collaboration with capable peers.[2] Finally, our exchanges reflect Carmichael Crutchfield's faith formation theory that emphasizes intergenerational encounters and that integrates racial/ethnic identity with Christian faith formation.[3]

Pray

Creator God, thank you for all the ways you manifest in the earth—in dance, in song, in art, and in time shared with family and friends just to laugh, to create memories and rituals and most of all to experience your sacred presence in the midst and in ourselves. Help me to continuously see your presence in the gifts given to humanity. Amen.

Act

As we spend time with the children in our lives, it is important to ask what they think, including what they think about spiritual matters, in what ways they see God, sense, perceive, or are reminded of sacred presence as they go throughout their day—in the walk to school, in an act of kindness, in their favorite movie, in the music, or in the time taken just to ask, "How was your day?"

Notes

1. John Dewey. *Democracy and Education: An Introduction to the Philosophy of Education* (Independently Published, 2021), Kindle Edition, Location 5978.

2. L. S. Vygotsky. *Mind in Society: The Development of Higher Psychological Processes* (Cambridge: Harvard University Press, 1978), 86.

3. Carmichael Crutchfield with Denise Janssen. *Pressing Forward Faith, Culture, and African American Youth* (Valley Forge: Judson Press Publishers, 2022), 114–115.

17

When Is God Coming to Houston?

MAI-ANH LE TRAN

Read

I dreaded talking about such topics as self-care, staying strong, and keeping the faith during the prolonged helplessness of the COVID-19 lockdown. I felt this way because of the harmful assumption that it requires nothing short of extraordinary moral character and personal aptitude to outlive global epidemiological and social catastrophe. However, in truth, I did experience and practice and grew in resilience through rather ordinary, pedestrian means. One such ordinary COVID activity was "Creative Corner" with my sister and then six-year-old niece, Amanda. Several times a week, initially at the whim of the restless child, we would have three-way FaceTime calls on our mobile phones—Amanda in Houston, my sister in Kansas City, and me in Chicago. Amanda would insist that we sit down and put our phones in front of us so that she could see that we were engaged with her and not checking work email. For at least thirty minutes to an hour, we would spend time coloring, drawing, painting, coming up with art challenges, playing pretend with finger puppets, and just yapping about this and that.

One day, as I was struggling to keep up with Amanda's tutorials for how to draw fruits, out of the blue, without looking up, she declared, "Cô Hai!" (That's what she calls me in Vietnamese, as I am "Auntie #2" to her within our extended family system.) "Cô Hai, when is God gonna come to Houston?!"

Even the best theologically trained academics do not always have the most brilliant responses when caught off guard. And those of us who know and care for children know that we cannot outsmart them, but we sure are going to give it a try anyway.

"Um . . . well . . . ," I stammered, "*why* do you ask?"

Without skipping a beat, and still working effortlessly with her colored pencil, Amanda stated matter-of-factly, "Because I want to talk to Him."

I could not have loved that child more in that moment. There she was, my little theologian, articulating her concrete operational theology of *incarnation*, in the only frame of reference and gender-specific notion of God that she knew, "When is God coming over for a conversation?" I bet she had some things to "reason with God" on that day.

Think

Within the context of my niece's intercultural and interfaith family, Amanda had been taught that God is everywhere, that if she wanted to talk to God, it's called prayer, and that she should close her eyes and recite the short prayers that her parents had taught her. But in that moment, the six-year-old flipped the script on her grown-ups, and she insisted that God had to "come over" to where she lives and be open to her embodied engagement. With the nimbleness of a fast-growing brain stimulated by art-filled play (as neuroscience has taught us), Amanda was able to make an imaginative leap from knowing perfunctorily that "prayer is what you say" to what theologians have written about for ages: that prayer is an attempt to open oneself up, from the depth of our animating passions and vulnerabilities, to the transcendent and the holy as we are facing the realities of our lives.

Amanda, with her eyes wide open, was "thinking her way through God's world." If nurtured in this way during her youth, she would grow into a spirituality in which she could wholly and simply be herself before God in this world. Such spirituality could mature into an active faith that is alert, not just to her own individual wishes and dreams, but to the joys and concerns about her world. If her questions could be encouraged and engaged seriously by adults, then this six-year-old would grow with eyes wide open to the ways in which one person's faith questions can lead to faithful practices that "resist in order to transform, to recreate the church as communal, sociable, healthy."

Pray

God, when are you coming over to our place today? Please come over to our place today. But you are already here, aren't you? Thank you.

Act

Make time to play as a spiritual practice with your children. Encourage curiosity, wonder, and questions. The curriculum focus here is not on biblical knowledge or faith statements. Rather, it is any and all things that make the child curious or concerned. Be prepared when they spring tough theological questions on you—and instead of dismissing those as inappropriate or inopportune, consider asking the child to invite God over for a conversation.

18

Story of Faith and Children

CHERYLE WALTERS RODRIGUEZ

Read

In 2002, while driving with my two children in the back seat of my car, my five-year-old son asked, "Mom, where do people come from?" As a practicing Buddhist for fourteen years, I explained the philosophy I learned as a Buddhist, which is that humans evolve from nature. The philosophy did not resonate with my son. Using the language of a kindergartener, he expressed dissatisfaction with my answer. I viewed his response as an answer to my spiritual conflict—should I continue practicing Buddhism, or should I seek the path of Christianity, where at that time, I felt my children would have more spiritual support? I chose to adopt the latter, which was the turning point of our family's faith walk. We began searching for a religious space that engaged with God.

I used this experience as a lesson—my children have spiritual wisdom that, when nurtured and honored, creates opportunities for them to learn and grow in faith. From that day on, I became intentional about listening and sharing their experiences. Their curiosity about nature opened the door to discussions about God's presence in creation. They developed a healthy appetite to explore God's creation with an eye for seeing relationships within creation and relationships between creation/nature and humankind.

Their spiritual wisdom and curiosity also guided our family on our journey to find a church home. We visited several churches and explored different denominations, based on the Spirit's leaning. Their experience gave them a broader understanding of different religious traditions. They respected various worship traditions, which enhanced their spiritual insight. Before going to bed, nighttime practices often included a conversation with God and references from stories in the Bible. The conversations and stories shared were relevant to my children's experiences.

Think

Honoring my children's feelings about their spiritual surroundings ultimately led us to a church where the spiritual leadership was rich with individuals who lived their faith. The church leadership, particularly the pastors (a husband-and-wife team), helped to provide direction about how to continue to flourish spiritually, as a natural part of daily life.

I learned to help my children to use many daily experiences as opportunities to further explore God's teachings. Now, as adults and parents, my children are each expressing their faith in their individual circles and teaching their children a love for God in ways that honor their children's spiritual curiosity and wisdom.

Pray

Awesome Creator, thank you for your presence that exists all around us. I pray that as I journey today, I remember to connect with you in all the ways you present your glorious love and power.

Act

As you are in nature with the children in your life, take the opportunity to use your senses to experience God's goodness in our created world. Celebrate together the things you can see and touch, taste, smell, and hear!

19

Bedtime Moments of Gratitude

NICOLE BROCATO

Read

At the end of each night, we say our bedtime prayers before we read our bedtime story. I ask my four-year-old, Rowan, to name three things he wants to thank God for. This gets him to think about things throughout his day or week that he has noticed and is grateful for. He has had some pretty funny answers—everything from his toy cars to a spoon for eating his ice cream, and some more tender-hearted answers like his baby sister and his Nana and Papa. One night, Rowan wanted to thank God for all the trees. I have noticed he is becoming more observant and asking if certain items or experiences can be listed in his prayers. On the day when he wanted to thank God for trees, we had gone to the Arboretum, a huge naturescape with a ton of trees, plants, and flowers. Just taking these few moments at bedtime when together we can name the things we are grateful for helps both of us focus more of our energy on gratitude throughout the day. It offers us a calming and joyful moment just before falling asleep when our hearts are full and our minds can rest in God's goodness.

Think

For many of us, gratitude is a key component of the way we want to teach our children to be in the world, and a way we understand and live out our faith. It is important that we not only model gratitude, but we invite our children into a personalized experience of thankfulness. As a caregiver, what are the ways you can show and elicit gratitude in your family? What behaviors can you show your children to take in and appreciate their surroundings?

Pray

Lord, I pray that my children always look closely and deeply at their surroundings, and find daily joy and a sense of peace. Help me to model gratefulness for the world you have created and for the relationships we enjoy.

Act

Cultivate a sense of gratitude in children (and yourself) by modeling and naming things you are grateful for together. Pray together with your children, thanking God for three things from the day for which you are thankful.

Section III
Storytelling

Our understanding of the Gospel is ultimately that of a powerful story about a caring God. Just as that narrative can call us into a life oriented toward the Divine, the stories we tell in our lives and about our lives represent compelling values, beliefs, and morals. In this section, contributors provide reflections on how shared storytelling moments provided opportunities for faith formation and how those stories connect us to the larger narrative of our faith.

20

Read to Raise Reflective Kids

ARCHANA SAMUEL

Read

Many of us have probably heard that "it takes a village to raise a child." I agree and add that it takes a library of books to raise a child, too. Children are curious and often ask many questions. When my son was young, I spent many hours reading a variety of books to him, including Bible books, stories, and biographies. Listening to the Bible and stories of faith-filled people motivated him a lot.

Recently, he graduated from high school and is now a student at the College of William and Mary. During his last Youth Sunday at church, he said, "I learned that life is given to us to love others and also to make sacrifices for each other." As a mom, I was excited to hear those beautiful words from him.

I have not only read to my own child, but to children at an elementary school near the church I pastor, to children in my home country of India, and every Sunday to the children where I served as the children's ministry director. Listening to words of faith and inspiration may help children reflect positively upon the stories they hear, and it may give them a perspective on faith and hope in life.

Think

Since the stories we read influence us in a variety of ways, we need to make intentional choices about what books we read to young children. What are the values that you want to instill in your children? Choose diverse books that encourage qualities like compassion and sharing.

Pray

God help us parents, primary caregivers, children, youth ministers, and all parental figures. Give us the heart and mind to read to the kids who are entrusted to us during our lives. Amen.

Act

Are we ready to engage our kids by reading and spending quality time with them? Spend some time today reading with the children in your life.

21

A Story

TAMAR WASOIAN

Read

"Is it a story about me?" a child asked as I began to tell a story at the preschool where I worked.

I love telling stories. I love making the stories come alive through my acting. What I love the most is sharing stories with children. I love seeing the children's eyes come wide open and their minds spinning, playing out the plot in their imagination. I can tell stories all day long. However, in the morning circle time, in small groups, and while we are walking is my best time. Then the story becomes about them individually simultaneously.

"Is it a story about me?" a child asks.

"Well, of course it is," I responded. Otherwise, it is not a good story, right? Stories are magical.

Think

Stories connect us through times and ages. Stories seem like they are imaginary, but in fact, they can be true encounters laced with our hopes and anticipations. Humans are neurologically bound to process the world around them in the form of stories. In telling a story, we put our experiences into meaningful narratives that transcend the here and now in connection with what is beyond the here and now.

Children with their boundless gifts of imagination connect well with stories. This connection between the real and the possible future is inseparable for children. When parents and caring adults affirm children's experiences through sharing stories, they build children's self-awareness and teach them how to be in the world.

Pray

In the beginning was the story, and our story begins with you. Help us see you in the arch-narrative of our lives and teach our children about your love for them.

Act

When your child is upset and/or misbehaving, sit next to them quietly and remind them to breathe deep as if they have a big balloon in their bellies. After a few of those deep breaths, share a little story about them affirming a positive act.

"Do you remember when I was sad, and you gave me a hug? It made me feel . . ."

Or "Once upon a time, there was a child who was upset about . . ."

It doesn't need to be a long story. A smile is guaranteed in just a few short sentences. A story works like magic all the time!

22

Nurturing Social and Sacred Conversations

ZANIQUE DAVIS

Read

When my son Zayn was about three months old, I created a bedtime routine for the family to reflect on our day, recite a Scripture, and pray. As the months progressed, Psalm 23 became a favorite and was consistent during our social yet sacred conversations. As I began to raise one of my favorite hymns or nursery rhymes, Zayn's eyes would glisten with joy and anticipation on hearing the Twenty-third Psalm being read. New nursery rhymes were created during these moments, and our phones were out of sight as we gave our undivided attention to be fully present in these divine moments. Our bedtime routine was not fixed but flexible based on the day's tasks. During these conversations, I have garnered insightful lessons on how he perceives the world around him and his understanding of God.

I vividly remember one night when Zayn offered his theological understanding of our beloved Twenty-third Psalm. He was three and a half years old at the time and attending preschool. On this night, as we began to recite each verse of the Psalm, he described the Lord as his friend, not his shepherd, as the text reads. Shepherd was a more complex concept that did not make sense for his three-year-old reality. Likewise, he shared how the Lord allows him to lay in his bed, look at his night light, and talk with his mom since he makes more sense of his place of comfort and safety as a bed instead of green pastures. Instead of being led by still waters, Zayn expressed how God gave him loving family and friends, reset his mind and body so that he could have fun with those people, and raise his awareness to help someone the next day.

Think

At that moment, I was startled by his response but also in awe of his ability to make sense of God through his lens. Instead of redirecting him to the original verbiage of the text, creating this non-judgmental space for him to share his perception validated his agency.

Knowing that his bedtime routine was flexible regarding what nursery rhymes were sung, which Scripture texts or books were read, and how much he wanted to share about his day gave him agency. Thus, this sense of belonging and agency made him feel comfortable understanding and expressing the Twenty-third Psalm in his own words. I am cognizant that, for many parents and caregivers, creating space for conversation during bedtime might be impossible or difficult. Hence, you could cultivate time for this nurturing to transpire at other times during the day. The important lesson is being intentional about allowing our children to actively participate, express their feelings, and feel validated in that shared space.

Pray

God, grant us the grace and fortitude to be faithful parents and caregivers as we endeavor to raise faithful children by creating transformative spaces for them to be cocreators in their faith formation.

Act

Through this act of cocreation, we recognize that our children embody God and the Spirit of God and have the innate agency to bring to fruition acts of faithfulness and sustainability for themselves and others. Cocreation helps us to embrace and make space for our children to function as partners in faith formation, as self-conscious social and sacred beings.

23

Enjoy the Journey

TOCCORO A. ARRINGTON

Read

I remember being alone in the doctor's office at the young age of eighteen, and the doctor telling me that I would never be able to have children. My disappointment and heartache were overwhelming. While I would not have children, I would eventually help to raise and parent a child. During my freshman year of college, I received an unexpected call from my mother telling me she was expecting a child. I was blessed to help welcome a sister into the family and to have a significant influence on her upbringing. It was an honor to be entrusted with her well-being. Many days, my prayer and confession sounded like, "There is no way I can do this without you, God." Today, she is a high school graduate attending an HBCU (Historically Black College and University) in the fall of 2023 on a full scholarship.

Think

Proverbs 22:6 (NIV) reads, "Start children off on the way they should go, and even when they are old, they will not turn from it." Vital is the word that comes to mind when I think about how faith plays an influential role in raising children. My own faith contributes to how I create the spaces for the faith of children to grow and develop. Based on my own experience, I helped provide a loving and nurturing environment that demonstrated unconditional love, grace, and mercy. My own faith helped me to manage difficult moments and conversations. My faith tells me that the Supreme Ruler will continue to open windows of opportunity for me to share my faith with youth and young adults and to encourage them to grow and develop into the men and women that they are called to be.

Pray

Dear Almighty, we thank you for your presence with us. You are the Creator of all good and perfect things. You have commanded us to be fruitful and multiply. Equip us now with the desire and determination to nurture children in a way that will bring glory and honor to your name. We pray for wisdom and knowledge to foster a cohesive bond between all generations. We thank you for the opportunity to provide a solid foundation of faith and to help every child explore and grow in their faith as they are being formed. This is our prayer. We believe that you are one who both hears and answers prayers. Amen and amen.

Act

When parents leave the hospital, they are not given a handbook on how to raise these new, unique human beings. Each birth begins a unique journey for the child and their family. While attending the Samuel Dewitt Proctor School of Theology, I often heard "Trust the process" and "Enjoy the journey." I say to you also, "trust the process" and "enjoy the journey." How might you trust the process of allowing faith to guide you in raising a child?

24

When Words Get in the Way

COLIN MCDONALD

Read

Halfway through our reading of the picture book that referred to "God" at every turn, without ever assigning an image or even an obvious cause and effect to what some refer to as God's omnipresence, a question dawned on my then two-year-old daughter. "Where is God?" she asked abruptly, if not for the fact that she had already waited twelve pages or more for the titular character in question to make an appearance. I stopped reading and laughed. Where, indeed, was God? With its tell-all, no-show style, this beautifully illustrated, well-meaning book had—from a young child's perspective, anyway—inadvertently broken the golden rule of storytelling. Our language with children works (or doesn't) this way, too, sometimes. When we find ourselves in a frenzy to communicate our faith adroitly and often, by necessity, succinctly, we lose sight of what we are so caught up and tongue-tied with trying to convey. So, where is God in our verbal and nonverbal presence with children?

Think

A quote hangs over my desk that reads, "I want to learn how to be the best receiver that I can ever be. Because I think graceful receiving is one of the most wonderful gifts we can give anybody."[1] Like its author, Fred Rogers, I am learning to quiet down inside and out, in an effort to receive. Typically, the older we are, and the more we have to give, our having can feel less like a resource than an imperative to reassert and self-correct (an almost nervous tic.) Not only as adults do we struggle to receive, but we writhe in fear of letting go, neglecting to accept a posture firm enough in faith to open and extend ourselves beyond stated belief.

Why should this matter? What difference does it make whether I learn to be the best receiver I can be when my ministry entails shepherding children and leading others on their trajectories of faith formation? And if not for the fact that children, when it comes to faith, are truly the best teachers, it might not. Yet every time a child interrupts a lesson plan or bedtime story to ask a question, they share their faith by way of expressing their needs. In the process, they teach us an invaluable lesson concerning the nature of value and grace. By admitting and acting on their needs instead of answers (including the need for some answers), children recall our shared and essential dependence on the grace of God. In this sense, it is children who are initiating dialogues concerned less with external, verifiable content and more verifiable felt experience, inviting and calling us out of our shells to rejoice in a recurring, spontaneous liturgy of renewal and exchange.

Pray

Creator God, I pray that in receiving all that children have to give, we might cocreate conditions, as opposed to compulsions, for sincere evaluation with the knowledge that sharing our faith is less a matter of instruction than acceptance.

Act

My daughter gave me the gift of graceful receiving in her need to know and experience more. In our time with children, whenever and wherever it comes to pass, we can receive the gifts of children by remembering our plan is only part of each day's lesson. Make space to attend to that which is felt in response to a Bible story or picture book, trusting that words will follow as needed. After reading, interrupt any immediate retention or reflection follow-up questions by asking everyone present, including other adults, to consider how the story made them feel.

Note

1. Fred Rogers, *You Are Special: Neighborly Words of Wisdom from Mister Rogers* (New York: Penguin Books, 1994).

25

God Is in My Mouth!

ASHLEY PRESCOTT BARLOW-THOMPSON

Read

The bustle of the day was coming to an end. Adam (my spouse) and I hastily prepared our dinner, and our very hungry preschooler was chowing down on his favorite meal of spaghetti and green beans. As was our dinner ritual each night, we played our favorite family dinner conversation starter: The Question Game. Each of us would take a turn asking a question about our days, our favorite things, or anything else.

"When was one time you were happy today?" asked Adam.

"When I played with Stella outside at school!" Prescott cheered.

"Right now! I am happy right now being with you!" I smiled.

"Me too. This is a happy part of my day and so was my coffee break with my staff!" Adam shared.

"Can you burp whenever you want?" Prescott giggled. I tried and failed. Adam got a little gas out.

"BURRRRRRP!" Prescott pretended in a loud voice.

"Where did you feel God with you today?" I asked.

"I knew you would ask that, Mommy!" Prescott rolled his eyes with a grin.

"I felt God with me today when I was stressed at work. I needed help, and I knew I wasn't alone," his dad shared.

"I felt God with me when I needed a break. I went outside and remembered God was with me in my heart as I walked," I commented.

"God was in your heart! They said that at Sunday School. God is *not* in my heart," Prescott said obstinately.

"God isn't in your heart?" I questioned curiously, trying to mask my theological concerns.

"Nope! God is in my mouth! That's where all the good stuff is!" he replied confidently with no religious concerns.

And this holy dinner conversation continued to deepen as we learned that Prescott finds God in his favorite foods, the kind and funny things he says, and the bubbles he blows with Stella on the playground. God was in the intimate details of his day, ever-present, bringing joy. And that was a good place for God to be!

Think

At the age of four, Prescott is still a concrete learner, and his brain is beginning to understand metaphor and the difference between physical reality and imagination. As he imagined God in his mouth, Prescott was expressing joy and wonder while connecting with big religious concepts: where is God? What is God up to in my life?

As mom to this curious, creative little one, it would have been easy for me to correct his answer, concerned that he doesn't understand God the way our faith tradition invites him to. After all, he is still in a stage of faith where he imitates the faith he sees in the adults around him.

Being present with my kid in the wonder, the curiosity, and the humor of this moment was primary to hearing more about the faith he was forming in real-time. By not giving a "correct" answer and by keeping my concerns to myself, there was space for him to elaborate, with his parents' guidance, questions, and support.

When we make space for the experience and the answers to come from our little ones, faith becomes more real for them, and we have the opportunity for our faith to be formed *by* them instead of simply being formed *for* them.

Pray

God of presence, thank you for the gifts of curiosity, joy, and creativity in our children. May we emulate them with our questions about faith and about you. Help us to meet them where they are and learn from them as they experience you in their hearts, mouths, and lives. Amen.

Act

Play The Question Game with your child today. Be open to whatever answers they give and questions they ask. Enjoy their experience of the world, just as they are, right now.

Section IV
Difficult Conversations

Any of us who spend considerable time with children
know they have a penchant for asking tough questions. While as adults we might be unsure about
their ability to comprehend the existential struggles
that our faith attempts to address, it is important to
honor the gravity and importance of these big questions. The following contributors provide reflections
on times when they have struggled together with the
children in their lives to attend to challenging and
sometimes overwhelming topics.

26

Connect before Correct

AMY HOWARD

Read

One might assume that as a pastor, I would have no trouble integrating faith development into the life of our family routine. However, I can assure you that the struggle is real. After my divorce, we found ourselves in survival mode, and daily faith development took an even further back seat; perhaps it was even hanging on the back bumper as tightly as possible trying not to fall off.

In the face of violent physical outbursts from one child and crippling panic attacks from the other, everyone around me had advice. I tried all of it, and everything seemed to escalate. I was at rock bottom, feeling as though I could not be the parent my children needed. Finally, I was given the best piece of advice: a contact for a counseling agency. With this agency, caregivers work with a parent coach while the children work with a licensed family counselor. Their target audience is children facing trauma and attachment struggles. It was the perfect fit for us.

I quickly learned a phrase that changed my parenting: "connect before correct." These three words have changed countless moments in our family, but most importantly, they have changed our moments of faith.

The three of us slept in the same bed every night, as they were not confident sleeping alone. As the moon began to rise, so did the anxiety within our house. The night hours for them have brought many terrors causing rest to be elusive. As an exhausted mom, I found myself growing frustrated as the evening approached, and by bedtime, I had no patience left. That is, until I remembered the three words "connect before correct." What if I established a new routine, one that is based on faith, shifting the narrative of the night?

I memorized Psalm 4:8: "I will lie down and sleep in peace, for you alone, O Lord, make me lie down in safety." When we lay down, I told them to repeat after me. We shared the verse and said our prayer, and I began to breathe deeply and slowly. They soon began to do the same. Terrors still plague some nights; however, we have a sweet moment of connection with each other and with God helping the anxiety of the night to shift just a bit.

Think

Children often have a limited emotional vocabulary. This is a hurdle when they do not know how to handle big emotions. As caregivers, we are often triggered by the words and actions displayed in those moments. We react instead of responding in a constructive way but choosing to "connect before correct" can be a helpful strategy. Centering ourselves equips us to connect with our children and help them feel safe and loved.

Pray

Gracious God, for the caregiver whose nights are restless, we pray for strength. You have shown us throughout Scripture how important rest is; help them rest and find renewed strength for their journey. Amen.

Act

Caregivers always face challenges. The busyness of the day creates hurdles for connection and intentional faith development. Don't overcomplicate things. Find one short verse of Scripture that speaks to your circumstance and utilize it. Never shy away from counseling and opportunities to seek encouragement as a caregiver.

27

Emerging Trust

RANDY CREATH

Read

It started as a lesson in inertia and became an experience in trust.

When a three-year-old pedals their tricycle as fast as they can and turns hard left, bad things happen. Her arm broke, and the neighborhood heard her screams at the terrified discovery of pain. As I gathered her into my arms, she tearfully pointed to the hard lump above her wrist. Her unspoken words were loud enough for me to hear, "It's not perfect anymore. Are you going to throw me away?" With gentle words and hugs, I assured her that I would never "throw her away."

In the hospital, she made it clear that the doctors and nurses were unknown to her and were therefore a threat. As I held her safe, they began telling her stories of their own broken bones and injuries, even showing scars. She began to be curious instead of terrified. Still, the moment of making her arm straight again was met with howls of horror at the pain. Putting the cast on it became another step in the process of reassurance. Even so, she did not leave my lap.

When we returned home, the pain made her concerned that she "was still broken." Later that evening when her older sister did something funny, she laughed. In mid-laugh, she looked at me and said, "Maybe it'll get better. I can't laugh if I'm too broken." She was beginning to understand that healing is a process that takes time.

The next dramatic step in this journey took place six weeks later when we went to have her cast removed. The doctor brought out a tool that looked a lot like one of my own electric wood saws. She shrieked in horror because one of her deepest fears was that she would have to have her arm cut off, and that fear came out in screams. Then, the doctor, a wise one if there ever was one, put the saw to his own arm and pulled the trigger. There was no blood, no bone, no fear on his face. He asked me to hold out my arm, and he repeated the process. Those small eyes, wide with fear, watched as nothing bad happened. Her fear began to slip further away. The cast was removed in a matter of minutes.

She looked at her arm. It was straight. She wiggled her fingers and thumb. They seemed to work just fine. A smile spread across her face. The fear was further forgotten.

On the way home, we got an ice cream cone. She asked, "Will I get an ice cream cone if I break my arm again?" I answered, "Every time, but please don't break your arm if you want ice cream." She giggled. The fear had passed. Trust was growing in new ways.

Think

To move from inertia to trust, my child needed help from all the adults around her. When each of us met her fear with understanding, listening, and patience, that broken arm was a vehicle that allowed her to learn that trust was possible and that she was important, even loved—ice cream loved. Each of her subsequent young life tragedies included fewer screams, more curiosity, and better attempts at trust. Had any of the adults mirrored her fear, the inertia of pain and injury would have held her back from the trust she so needed to learn.

Pray

Creator God, when arms break and fear rises, let the helpers be listeners and healers, so that trust may be restored.

Act

As a parent or caregiver, your fear is like gasoline when added to the fear of a child. Your gentle, warm presence is the reassurance that brings healing and hope to the young and malleable children in your care. Learn to manage your own fear, and yours will not magnify the fear of those little ones.

28

"Grandma, I don't want to die!"

VIRGINIA A. LEE

Read

"Grandma, I don't want to die!" In tears, my niece uttered those words in despair to my mother and her grandmother.

My mother knew, from years of experience, to ask more questions. "What happened? What made you think about dying?"

My niece responded, "My Sunday school teacher said I had to give my heart to Jesus!"

In her five-year-old mind, giving her heart away meant someone cutting her chest open and pulling out her heart, which she rightly deduced would make her die. Grandma Eva explained that what her Sunday school teacher meant was that she should love Jesus with all her heart; that it did not mean she had to physically hand her heart to Jesus. After more conversation and a hug from Grandma Eva, my niece was reassured.

Think

Young children think in concrete terms. You may have seen a meme or a video with a young child trying to hit a ball off a tee, and when they keep missing it, they are told to keep their eye on the ball. Adults know that means to watch the ball closely, but a young child will often move to the ball and physically put their eye on it. Later, children will learn abstract and metaphorical language, but when they are young, they think about things concretely.

My niece loved her Sunday school teachers and trusted them, which is probably why she was so distressed about what she thought they wanted her to do. She was afraid and needed someone with whom she could talk.

While I think we need to remember to use language that is appropriate for the age and maturity of the child, I am not reprimanding the Sunday school teachers. I have been teaching about concepts like these for many years, and yet sometimes, I need to be reminded by children that we all forget and make mistakes! Just recently, I was talking with my great-nieces about the summer solstice. I said that it was the longest day of the year.

My eight-year-old niece looked at me with a quizzical look and said, "'Ginia, how do they do that?"

I suddenly realized that she was trying to figure out how a twenty-four-hour day could be longer than another. I told her: "That is a great question, and actually, I said it the wrong way. What I meant to say was that on the summer solstice, we had the longest amount of sunlight—that the daylight was longer than the night." I asked if she remembered that in the winter the nights were longer than the daylight, and that was one of the differences between summer and winter. Her face changed to one of understanding, and we talked some more about what it meant to be in the season of summer.

Both encounters illustrate the importance of a child feeling comfortable asking questions. It is equally important that the adult hears and listens to the child's questions and actively engages in conversation. It is not about always saying the right thing or knowing all the answers. Rather, we need to be available as good listeners, engaging in conversations about questions of importance to children. One good response to many questions is, "What do you think?"

That is theological reflection, and it is a major part of faith formation.

Pray

Gracious God, you are always ready to hear my questions in times of joy or distress. Help me hear the questions of children, really listen to what they are asking, and be willing to engage them in conversation around the topics that are important to them. Amen.

Act

Pay attention to the questions and concerns of children. They usually occur when you are busy or when you least expect them. They are hard to schedule. Recognize them as holy moments of faith formation. (Not all "faith formation" takes place in churches! Actually, much of it takes place in daily interactions.) Don't worry; it is not about having the right answers. It is about hearing, listening, and taking seriously the questions and concerns. It is about conversation.

29

Openness

BETHANY WHERRY

Read

My niece Amaya (age 8) and nephew Alex (age 7) often spend weekends with my parents and me at my parents' home. My favorite part of every hangout is talking with them. They think very deeply, so it is not surprising that their questions can sometimes exhaust the adults. I often step in to have crucial conversations with my little loves.

During a weekend hangout, they were watching YouTube videos when Alex became noticeably quiet and stared at one of my parents' paintings on the wall: a collage of The Passion of Christ. I asked what he was thinking. He said, "Auntie, is that a picture of Jesus dying on the cross? Why did they do that? Couldn't they just leave him alone?" This, of course, sparked questions for Amaya as well.

With a grateful heart for their thirst for knowledge, I said that Christ was a radical. He was different. That idea piqued their interest. They are both experiencing that feeling of *otherness* at school. I went on to explain, "Jesus had bullies just like you do. His bullies were very selfish and powerful priests who thought his message would take away from their power. They conspired with the government and convinced one of

Jesus' disciples, a friend, to betray him." They wondered why Jesus would *choose* such a friend. "To be sure he fulfilled his purpose on earth," I explained. "God knew when Jesus was born that death was part of that purpose. When Jesus died, he went to hell, won the battle over death, was raised to life on earth, and ascended into heaven. That's why, when we die, we can go to heaven to be with God. Jesus died so our souls could have eternal life in heaven."

Amaya nodded intently. Then she asked, "If Jesus fought so we could all go to heaven, does that mean *everyone* gets to go to heaven? Did his *bullies* get to go to heaven?" Smiling at the depth of thought, I took the opportunity to talk about the Christian walk. We talked about what a disciple is, what the word *Christian* means, and how that governs how we should live. Finally, I said, "It's simple: if you live your life focused on sharing the love of God, living like Christ, and loving your neighbor like yourself, you're on a great path to heaven!" After a moment of silence, Alex said, "Sounds good. I can do that!" That day, they decided they wanted to go to heaven so they could see and be with our loved ones who had passed away and (hopefully) gone to heaven. They wanted to meet Jesus for themselves.

Think

Children respond to openness. They are little sponges. You are their safe space, so be open and available to answer their questions. Use language that is accessible to them. Rather than quoting a King James Version verse such as "He was wounded for our transgressions" (Isaiah 53:5-8 KJV), try saying, "He took those beatings so we wouldn't have to." Don't be afraid to tackle the hard concepts of faith: the Crucifixion, sin, hell, etc. They can handle difficult conversations. Your job when having those conversations is to provide information, and then give them hope and tools to move in the world. Make connections to their lived experience and current understanding of the world. While talking, actively think about things they have experienced, concepts you have already discussed, and perceptions they already have. So many faith concepts can be intangible, and children need tangible things to connect to.

Pray

Dear God, giver of all knowledge, create in me a spirit of openness and love. Help me to bring my knowledge and faith in you to the table when children yearn to learn about you. Allow me to see the world through the eyes of a child to better understand how to lead them to you. May my words edify even the smallest of souls. In the name of Jesus the Christ, amen.

Act

Not every faith conversation happens in the church setting, so try different approaches. Watch a movie with your child that tells a biblical story. Plan enough time to pause the movie and answer questions that might arise from the plot of the story.

30

Responding to Tough Questions

KAREN-MARIE YUST

Read

We were driving home from a Good Friday service when my eight-year-old asked, "Why did God let Chrissy (a fictitious name) get cancer?" Her friend was receiving chemotherapy for leukemia, and we prayed regularly for healing.

"God feels sad that Chrissy is sick," I replied. "Our bodies are pretty strong, but sometimes they have a hard time fighting off germs and other things that make us sick. God wants Chrissy to get well as much as we do."

"But why doesn't God just make her well?" she persisted. In her voice, I heard fear and anger, as well as concern for her friend.

"God relies on smart doctors and nurses and researchers to help people get well," I responded. "God knows that all the people around Chrissy are taking care of her and showing her how much she is loved. That helps her body fight harder to get rid of the bad cells and make new, healthy cells."

My daughter pondered my words for a few minutes, then said, "So when I go over to Chrissy's house to play, it helps her get better?"

"Absolutely!" was my emphatic response.

"And when we pray for the doctors and nurses to do their best to help her, that's good, too?" she asked.

"Yes, I think it makes a difference," I said.

Another minute passed, and she declared: "I'm going to see if Chrissy can play after the Easter Egg Hunt tomorrow."

"Good idea," I replied, and my daughter went back to looking out the car window.

Think

Talking with children about serious illnesses, death, natural disasters, school shootings, and other kinds of trauma is tough. Yet child development experts have found that kids process difficult situations better when they are encouraged to ask questions and given basic information in response. Information calms fears because it takes away the feeling of not knowing what is going on. Think about how you feel when you encounter a situation you do not understand. Without reliable information, you might imagine all kinds of wild and scary scenarios, triggering a fight-flight-freeze response. Children react similarly by acting out (fight), withdrawing (flight), or going over the situation again and again (freeze). Encouraging them to ask questions and giving simple, honest answers offers them an opportunity to reflect faithfully with a trusted adult on what is troubling them.

Pray

God, you are our companion in all that happens. You are with us when children get sick. You share our pain when trauma threatens to overwhelm our loved ones. And you help us find words to say when kids ask hard questions. Thank you. Amen.

Act

It is easier to talk about big things if we already have a Q&A routine established around little things. Invite kids to share something that upset them recently. Then ask, "How did you feel when that happened?" "What questions do you have that I might help you answer?" If they ask about something you don't know, research answers together.

31

Feeling Big Feelings

JUSTIN THORNBURGH

Read

My wife and kids are five hundred miles away visiting her parents. I am sitting on our couch with my phone, video-chatting with them.

"Hey guys," I said, my voice catching. "Mom and I were hoping this could have waited until you all got home, but unfortunately it can't. Nara (our thirteen-year-old dog) has been really, really sick these last few days and, like we did with Malcolm (our other dog who died several years ago), we are going to have to say goodbye. We hope she will make it until you get home, but we can't promise that. I'm so, so sorry we had to tell you like this."

My twelve-year-old puts on a strong face though I can see tears stream down his cheeks. As I explain to my four-year-old what this means, his heart breaks in real time. My eight-year-old will not know until later because he is away at church camp. As the kids process this, mom wraps her arms around them both, and we sit silently as the tears flow.

Think

"To everything there is a season." As cliche as this phrase seems at times, I find it a great comfort in times such as described above. So often, in an effort to shield and protect, we want to rush past these difficult moments and give words of encouragement, but I really have come to believe that we should allow these moments the sacredness they deserve and not rush past them because they are uncomfortable for us.

Grief is something we all experience, and we all process it differently. It is important to give our kids the space they need to fully experience that grief. We can do this without deflecting and diminishing their feelings by just being present for them, not rushing to helpful words, and being there to answer questions they might have.

As adults, we have been conditioned to hide our feelings, especially grief. My friend Angela, who is a death doula specializing in helping adults learn to talk to kids about death, says, "Holding space for kids means allowing them to express and feel. Model the container they need to create for themselves. In that is healing for all." I have found in my own work as a pastor and a parent that these words ring true. When I can show my breadth of feelings, it allows kids to see that it is okay. Even more importantly, they can understand that they are not feeling those feelings alone, and in that shared experience, healing will come.

Pray

God, who laughed and danced at the wedding, and who wept at the tomb of your dear friend, thank you for giving us the fullness of our emotions. In all the seasons of our days, help us to experience them fully just as you have.

Act

I encourage you to just sit with your kiddos when their emotions are big. I know it can be difficult as it can trigger things within us, but I find that as I do this, they are helping me to heal as well.

32

A Very Dark Night

TAMAR WASOIAN

Read

We were walking to the assembly hall for the after-dinner gathering when we lost electricity. The assembly hall was a separate building from the dining hall, and each camp leader walked with their assigned group of children. This night happened a few years after the end of the civil war in Lebanon, and a power outage was considered normal. The children's camp was in the countryside, and it was very dark even when the lights were on.

As the power went off, countless bright stars became visible in the sky. Coming from a big and bright city, I was mesmerized by the dark sky adorned with glittering stars. Trying to engage the children with this breathtaking experience, I said, "Children, look at how beautiful and bright God created the stars!"

One child lifted her head up and after a brief pause said, "Why would God create all these stars? What would we do if they fell on our head?"

Think

I always remember this experience as if it happened today. Back then, I did not understand why she said this, but it became a formative experience that taught me not to take children and their experiences for granted. This child survived the trauma of war and bombs falling from the sky on her head all her life. I grew up in a country that did not experience war as she had. In her experience, bright things in the sky fell down, made loud noises, and scared her. She needed to hide to be safe, and her question was very valid. "Why did God create stars and rockets if they can fall down and hurt?" She could not make sense of the trauma of war and falling bombs. Underneath her question was a deeper question about God that she did not know how to express.

Pray

Our heavenly Parent, help us learn how to
  listen to each other.
Grant us wisdom to learn genuine and honest
  questioning from our children.
Help us nurture them in their faithful curiosity
  to grow in knowing you.

Act

Children know and internalize experiences more than we think they do. Talk with them and engage with them about their experiences. Help them learn how to express their worries and fears so we can respond to open-ended statements about the situation. This provides the space for conversation where feelings can be expressed and processed.

33

Raising Anti-Racist Children

PAULA CRIPPS-VALLEJO

Read

When my eldest child was seven years old, she had set aside phone time to play games. After a few minutes, she sighed deeply and said, "Oh no."

Without thinking too deeply, I said, "Oh baby, did the phone glitch again?"

And she replied, "No, I am just so tired of only seeing white characters and hands." She wondered aloud in frustration why the characters in her favorite game were never her light brown color, her papi's dark brown color, or even her abuela's beautiful black skin color.

As a white woman who is married to an Afro-Latino man, and as a faith leader who has been honored to pastor primarily Latinx communities, I see firsthand how covert and overt racism shows up in our daily lives. I also see moments that should be filled with relaxation and joy, such as playing a phone game, turn into moments where my children and my faith family are considered other.

Think

I am reminded of the importance of supporting my children as they face the continual micro-aggressions of racism many times daily. Helping my children know their sacred worth with my words and actions is one way I am intentional about supporting them. Surrounding them with family and friends of many ethnicities and races, including other children who look like them, is another way our family is intentional about raising anti-racist children. In reality, my children are probably more used to the daily effects of racism than I am. My daughter looked me in the eyes and said, "I know things will change. It's just so frustrating."

Pray

God, who created each and every one of your children in your image, we lament how racism interferes with our days, our play, our children, and our world. Guide us to be truly anti-racist in all that we say and do. Turn our deep sighs of frustration into the joy and laughter of a child!

Act

I suggest that the first step in raising anti-racist children is talking with them about the reality of systemic racism and naming it when we see it, including in ourselves and our assumptions. Notice together the privilege of some people to not have to deal with racism every day, and name how it is wrong that anyone should ever feel less than. Intentionally choose books, videos, music, and movies that engage and celebrate cultures other than your own. Take the first steps. Do something.

34

Parents Talking about Human Sexuality

CARMICHAEL D. CRUTCHFIELD

Read

A parishioner, whom I will call Frank, came to me one day concerned that he had done something wrong as a father and as a result, his children had "become homosexual." His daughter from a previous marriage was not a member of the church where I served as pastor; therefore, I only knew her from a distance. But I did know several years prior to my present conversation with her father she had come out, letting people know she was a lesbian.

Frank's son was raised in what we might refer to as a "Christian home" and was active in the church I served. Frank and his wife saw to it that their children attended all the spiritual enrichment classes offered in his community. As a matter of fact, Frank's son was sometimes so involved in spiritual events outside of his home church that he did not always participate in the church's youth group. The son was extremely intelligent and talented and was offered several academic and artistic scholarships across the country. He chose to go to a college in a city located in the northern part of the United States.

Not long after having been away at school, Frank's son let his parents know he had a male companion and was now acknowledging himself as gay. This devastated his parents to the point that Frank came to me for counseling. Frank calmly told me how disappointed he was and blamed himself for possibly failing to nurture his children properly.

Think

My conversation with Frank reminded me of a class I had taken at seminary on human sexuality. In that class, I came to grips with the silence about human sexuality in the churches where I had served as pastor or been a member. Although I have been a member of the same denomination all my life, conversations with many others gave me cause to believe the silence about human sexuality is not my unique experience in the church.

Furthermore, my experience with Frank gives rise to the question of how Black parents are equipped to talk to their children about human sexuality and gender identity. How do we go beyond myths, incorrect reading of the Bible, and miseducation to help our children be accepting of themselves? How do we support parents in developing a better understanding of sexuality and sexual attraction?

Pray

Creator of all human life, open our hearts and minds to your love and care for all of humanity. Help your people to overcome inadequate teaching that leads to prejudice and discrimination. Continue to help us to have clean hearts so that we might serve you.

Act

With the help of your pastor, members of your church, or your own friends, form a small group of people to find resources on the church and human sexuality. Look for the works of authors such as Emilie Townes and Kelly Brown Douglas.

35

Instilling Faith as a Caregiver

CINDY A. CUMMINS

Read

Becoming a caregiver to a child brings a responsibility unmatched by any other. The incorporation of faith in the task of raising a child can be overwhelming, as we tend to place so many expectations on ourselves as caregivers to do it perfectly. As a new mom to my daughters who joined me through adoption from China, I defaulted to what I knew about my own faith and my style of living out that faith: simplistic, consistent, and inclusive.

As children, my daughters were a part of a church program that offered the fundamentals of Christian education. If asked, they would tell you it was things we dealt with together that made them choose to continue exploring faith. Simple childlike things like saying a prayer when you see an ambulance or learning about the steps of the Easter story through Resurrection eggs impacted them. Catching caterpillars and watching them transform into butterflies brought discussions of God's creativity and power. Watching sunsets and sunrises and looking for dew drops on blades of grass or flowers taught them to notice God's beauty is constant and available to find every single day if we take the time to notice.

Because they were Chinese and I was not (nor was I married), sometimes we had difficult conversations after they were made aware of these differences through a playground incident. It was here that inclusivity was brought into the picture as I reminded them that God asks us to love others, period. There are not any subheadings to God's description of others, so I tried to instill in my girls that we are not God and cannot add requirements. This is true regardless of whether those others look differently, act unlike us, choose to express themselves in ways we may not understand, or even if they hurt us purposely, we try our hardest to love them. My daughters are now fifteen and twenty-one, and both have established a faith of their own, which is what I emphasized all along: God and you have the relationship, not your mom, God, and you. We found the answers together.

Think

When each girl, at different ages, chose not to attend church with me, I did not see these moments as failures. Rather, it was an affirmation of what I wanted for them, which was to find who they are with God and establish that relationship themselves. I guided if asked. I added questions for them to consider on their journey. My oldest told me the thing she liked best about this style was that I was not legalistic in my approach, saying it was my way or nothing. My youngest said she appreciated that I never judged their questions, even if they were hard for them to ask. Did I do it right? Who knows. Did others judge my style? Of course. However, the results I see in my daughters tell me I did okay.

Pray

God, help us use the opportunities you bring us as caregivers to learn, teach, and grow in our faith. May we allow you to be the guide on the journey's path through the peaks and valleys.

Act

I hold firmly to the belief that we want to be heard as individuals. This does not start when adulthood hits. It starts when that toddler begins to verbalize their own wants and desires. Letting my daughters form their own opinions and voice them to me honestly made them feel heard. It let me into who they were becoming, and whether I agreed or not, I wanted to listen and hear them as I feel Jesus would with anyone who spoke with him about beliefs, questions, issues, or wisdom in decisions. I know I could have made my girls stay at my church against their wishes. Although it hurt my heart due to my love for my church, ultimately, it gave them assurance that what God was teaching them individually mattered and I wanted to honor it. Listen to your child. Hear what they need.

36

God's Provision of Church Family as Extended Family

HILARY OHRT

Read

As humans, we are navigating a world that is full of pain, suffering, and sadness. This can also be mirrored by difficult dynamics in family life. Financial stressors, employment stressors, extended family dynamics, or differences of opinion in childrearing are all factors that can challenge daily life for a family. Children experience both the intended and unintended consequences of choices made by adult caregivers. At the same time, children are navigating their own experiences in the world separate from the family unit. The world is a big, confusing, and potentially scary place if we are not secure in ourselves as children of God. Our faith is one of the tools that help us navigate this unpredictable world and make it feel a little more manageable.

Think

Hebrews 10:24-25 states, "And let us consider how to provoke one another to love and good deeds, not neglecting to meet together, as is the habit of some, but encouraging one another, and all the more as you see the Day approaching."

Engaging in church family life is one way God provides refuge and strength through support, encouragement, and teaching for each of us as followers. Consistent attendance at church and church activities allows for security in the routine, and structure allows relationships to form that support both the adults and the children and the family unit. This broader family support system exists to fill in the gap when we as adults struggle to navigate worldly life as parents. Participation in faith communities helps parents and children to have additional networks of encouragement and guidance.

Pray

Lord, as human individuals, we can struggle to find our way. When we are lost, we ask that you show us the way. We know that we can never accurately see the future, but we can trust that, daily, you are guiding us along the path you have designed for us. When we fall, we know you will pick us up and put us back on the road. Help us rest securely in you.

Act

Prioritize engagement in church family life. This will provide opportunities for learning, encouragement, and shared experience with God as the foundation. If finding a church family is challenging, ask God to open the door and show the way.

37

Teaching by What We Leave Out

ERIN S. KEYES

Read

When I think about raising faithful children or children in general, I often focus on parents, grandparents, aunts, uncles, and godparents. But there is an overlooked group—the teachers. As caretakers responsible for raising faithful children, they hold significant sway over our children's lives, shaping their perspectives and actions. I am fortunate to be both a teacher by profession and a parent by grace, giving me the opportunity to influence the world as seen through the eyes of children who are learners with me. Sadly, as adults, we sometimes fail to listen and learn from the younger ones around us.

During my time as a third-grade teacher in a private Christian school, we used a popular evangelical mainstream curriculum, rich with pictures depicting lofty religious ideas that surpass our adult understanding. One day, while discussing heaven, a student raised their hand and asked in a worried tone, "Will I get to go to heaven?"

My reply was, "Of course you'll be able to go to heaven. Why do you ask?"

This question shattered my heart and became a pivotal moment that shaped my teaching and parenting philosophy.

This sweet, innocent child questioned their place in heaven because "there's no one in that picture (representing heaven) that even looks like me." They felt excluded from what they understood as my depiction of heaven. I felt a profound responsibility to rectify this perception, ensuring they knew God loved them as deeply and immeasurably as any of those people in the photo. How could I, as the adult in this moment, overseeing their social, emotional, spiritual, and physical development, have overlooked this crucial aspect? As their teacher and one who, like this student, also encounters the world in a brown body, I can and must pay attention to helping students feel seen and represented in a world that too often fails to represent them fully as beloved children in the image of God.

Think

As both a teacher and parent entrusted with raising children to be loving, compassionate, and empathetic, I am reminded that my actions hold more weight than my words. Our collective actions speak louder than our words. How can I use my adult voice to ensure that all children are represented as created in the image of God with sacred worth?

Pray

Most faithful God, as we interact with the children you have entrusted to us, remind us that what they see carries more significance than what they hear. Help us to join in your work of creating more just spaces for all people to know themselves as your beloved. Grant us the grace to be faithful stewards over our actions, continually nurturing faithful children. Thank you. Asé and amen.

Act

As you interact with the younger generation, pay attention to the messages they are receiving in the ways our world represents them in relation to others and God. We have a responsibility to ensure that children see and know that all people are beloved by God by helping them see God in the many and various peoples of the world. Today, whether through a book, a conversation, or your interaction with others, in ways both spoken and enacted, ensure that children see and know that they and all people are loved by God.

38

Parenting Through a Pandemic

TIFFANY P. HARRIS-GREENE

Read

Faith over fear. That slogan was everywhere throughout the pandemic. I saw it on different types of apparel and too many times across social media platforms. It is a catchy phrase that carries a heavy message. I wanted my faith to be over my fear in March 2020, when the outside world shut down with little to no notice. The risk of unprecedented sickness and death was in every breath that we took outside of our homes. I wanted the faith that I believed I had to replace the paralyzing fear that I felt. But in that moment, amid a global change, my fear was over my faith, and I still had to parent. I had to show up for my children while trying to figure out how to show up for myself.

Parenting in a pandemic showed me that my vulnerabilities were teaching moments for my children. My example carried more weight than my words. I am certain this has always been true, but the pandemic provided restricted space for this truth to be illuminated. When I was overwhelmed, I explained why I needed ten minutes to myself. Those times I was deep breathing while walking through grocery stores, I shared why I had to focus and apologized if I was curt.

Anxiously purchasing masks, hand sanitizer, and disinfectants facilitated a conversation around being prayerful and prepared. We stopped saying "new normal" and allowed life to be a new adventure. In sharing my vulnerabilities and not asking my children to interpret them, a culture of open communication within our family became normative.

Think

I found that acknowledging the fear was uncomfortable and necessary. It was uncomfortable because the trusted adults of my childhood were always strong. I equated fear with weakness. However, my belief that a declaration of strength served as a demonstration of faith was disproven; this was important learning for me. Faith was not limited to strength. Faith showed up by waking up each day, doing my best as a parent, without knowing the outcome of my best. Faith was acknowledging my fear instead of ignoring it. Allowing my children to ask questions that did not have obvious answers helped them. They were able to settle into their own faith because answers are not always available and that was a lesson of their lived experience.

Pray

God, help me to lovingly see me so that I may lovingly see my child(ren). Help me to be empathetic and not indifferent to their needs.

Act

For parents who want to help their children develop faith, I encourage them to have conversations about what faith looks like. Discuss moments in their lives where they had to have faith because the outcome was uncertain. Start at their developmental and emotional level. Talk about working toward a goal because they believe in achieving that goal. Then, let them see it. Let them see faith in action. My children experienced my parenting through a pandemic. Learning to modify my parenting during the pandemic was a demonstration of my faith.

39

Navigating Separation and Divorce

JEFFREY A. HOWARD

Read

"Oh man, I wish I could stay with you forever, Daddy. Do I have to go back with her (mom)?" These words were from my six-year-old daughter Elizabeth, whom I affectionately nicknamed Ladybug. She is a preacher's kid; I am a full-time staff pastor at my local church. Her mom and I have known each other for over seventeen years. We dated for six years and were happily married for seven years. Ultimately, my decision to go into ministry ended our relationship. As you can imagine, separation and divorce can become ugly in some situations. Trying to co-parent can be even harder, especially from another state. Additionally, the kids become innocent casualties and suffer the most.

Memoirist, poet, and civil rights activist Maya Angelou once wrote that she became the kind of parent her parents were to her. My mother had me at an early age and was forced to give up her dreams. Throughout her life, she faced challenges but always instilled in me to keep God first, never letting anything stop me. It was that blueprint that helped me navigate during the separation and divorce. Though my daughter stays in another state, I made extra efforts weekly to take my daughter out on dates, pick her up after school to do homework, and mani/pedi sessions, our personal favorite activity together. I have watched the light in my daughter's eyes blaze when I surprised her with lunch dates in her cafeteria. We go over daily affirmations, and we pray together. In spite of our family situation, she knows she is loved and supported, and I believe that knowledge has made a huge difference in her life.

Think

If you are facing a situation like mine or know of someone who is, refer the person or family to counseling. I was able to be a healthy parent to my daughter because I made the decision to go see a trained counselor. It is okay to go sit on someone's couch. I am able to co-parent with my ex-wife, and our daughter gets to see both of us. Our daughter gets to experience both parents at our best. Whether the separation and divorce are pending or have already happened, we still have a responsibility to our child(ren) as parents. They are watching, and they feel every bit of the situation. We are obliged to offer our children a new path forward. With prayer, daily Scripture reading, and sitting on someone's couch, you can do all things through Christ who will give you strength.

Pray

God, grant the reader a peace of mind in knowing that despite their present situation, you are with them. I pray for their family situation, that they have a healthy path forward in being able to raise their child(ren) in difficult situations, and that you provide resources to help them navigate.

Act

Do you know anyone who is separated or divorced and has children? Ask a few parents who co-parent about the challenges and joys of co-parenting.

40

When Children are Sick

TERESA E. SNORTON

Read

Both of my sons, my niece, and the two daughters of my neighbor had chicken pox at the same time. They spent a lot of time together playing, so it was no surprise that they passed the disease around among themselves in the span of a few days. My oldest son, who was about eight years old at the time, had the worst case of all the children. He had blisters all over his body, and they itched. He was miserable!

One night as I put him to bed, he looked up at me and said "Mama, I feel so bad! Am I dying?" I knew he was in pain and extremely uncomfortable, but I was totally unprepared for his question about his own mortality. I did not expect an eight-year-old to leap into such deep and profound ponderings. I assured him that he was not dying, and then seemingly relieved, he asked me to pray for him. My heart leaped that, at his age, he was mindful of prayer and the power it had in connecting him to the eternal source and Creator, God. My mind was grieved that I, as the parent, had not been the one to suggest prayer to him.

Think

This experience taught me to always remember the resource of prayer when working with children. Children get the flu, COVID, colds, cancer, and other diseases. They break bones, skin their knees, and get teeth knocked out in sports or daredevil activities. These are the times that parents and caregivers can use to cultivate the practice of prayer with children. The prayer does not have to be long and complicated, and the illness or injury does not have to be life-threatening. But surely, this practice becomes a powerful reminder that talking to God—whatever our need or condition—is always in order.

When was the last time you prayed with your child when he/she was hurt, sick, or in distress? Has your child seen you pray when you were hurt, sick, or in distress? Children learn so much from what they see. When we practice the faithful act of prayer in their presence, we are modeling what it means to believe and to trust in God for all our needs.

Pray

Creator God, help us to remember to pray for and with our children, especially when they hurt. Help us to remember to pray in front of our children so that our faith is evident and alive right in front of their lives.

Act

The next time a child in your life gets hurt, sick, or feels bad, gather all the children and adults together and pray with the one whose body, mind, or spirit is troubled.

41

Naming How Faith Impacts Our Choices

EMILY A. PECK

Read

My dishwasher broke. This happens; it is part of life. Once I found out that replacing the entire thing made more practical sense than repairing it, I decided I would, indeed, replace it. I put it in the category of "being a homeowner"—well, a home-owner who is a single mom who does not want to do dishes by hand and is lucky enough to have saved enough money in an emergency savings account for something like this.

Delivery was delayed. Supply chain issues, holiday sched-ules, whatever the reason, I was going to be without a dish-washer for two weeks. I declared to the kids that we were going to use paper plates and plasticware. Predictably, my youngest child (who was five at the time) said, "But Mama! That's bad for the earth!" He was right, of course. I have spent time teaching the kids about earth care as part of the practice of our Christian faith. This was an aspect of his faith formation that had been effective. Of course, the effectiveness showed up right then I was wishing it was not so effective. I did not want to do all those dishes!

Think

Sometimes Christian practices fit easily with the way we are already living our lives. Sometimes they do not. In my house, we explicitly talk about the things we do because of our faith. We go to church because it is important to worship and learn about God in community. I grew up with cloth napkins; it has been easy to keep using cloth napkins as a way to care for the earth as a parent. As a Christian, I have taught my kids that we do this, not because it is how I grew up, but because my faith says it is a good way to practice creation care. God gave humanity the task of caring for the planet during creation.

Ellen Davis, Professor of Bible and Practical Theology at Duke Divinity School, said in an episode of the *On Being* podcast that translating words differently can help us to relate to creation differently. In Genesis 1, the Bible says that humans are to have "dominion" over the creatures (verses 26 and 28) and to "subdue" the earth (also verse 28). Davis, however, translates it differently. She said in that podcast, "I render it 'exercise skilled mastery amongst the creatures' because I think the notion of skilled mastery suggests something like a craft, an art, of being human . . . But the condition for our exercise of skilled mastery is set by the prior blessing of the creatures of sea and sky that they are to be fruitful and multiply. So, whatever it means for us to exercise skilled mastery, it cannot undo that prior blessing."[1]

Pray

Creator God, help us find ways to exercise the art of being human that continues and does not undo your blessing of all creation. Amen.

Act

Choose one new thing your family can do together that helps care for the planet. Some possibilities might be picking up litter on a nearby road, starting to compost, or collecting rainwater to use to water indoor plants. As you make your decision, talk about how this is part of the art of being humans created by God to help bless God's creation.

Note

1. "Wendell Berry and Ellen Davis: The Art of Being Creatures." The On Being Project, Original Air Date: June 10, 2010; updated April 16, 2020. https://onbeing. org/programs/wendell-berry-ellen-davis-the-art-of-being-creatures/. Special thanks to Fred Edie for pointing me to this particular episode in connection with creation care.

42

Trisagion

JENNY HADDAD MOSHER

Read

We have traveled back to our home parish where all the boys were baptized, Holy Transfiguration Orthodox Church, to say goodbye to sweet Bob, who lived, amazingly, to 102. My two sons sing with their father in the choir. My teen son stands with me in the packed nave, our arms around one another. The funeral liturgy, the eulogy, the Last Kiss—all offered with tangible thanksgiving for a life so well lived—and then the casket is closed, and we are on our way to the cemetery. We will bury Bob alongside Vera, his wife, and Anna and Betty, Vera's two sisters. After sharing a household for fifty years, they will now share a plot.

Such salt of the earth, these elders. So many small concrete acts of care and delight—sneaking treats to the boys, recruiting them to tasks in the parish kitchen, shielding them from grumpy fellow parishioners, always with bright smiles. They built a world of unambiguous welcome for my sons, and I am so grateful. Because Bob filled our lives with so much love, we are here to say goodbye, face to face, not keeping ourselves from the keen sadness that comes with seeing him lying lifeless in our midst. As his casket is lowered into the earth, we sing, as we sang alongside him so many times in life:

Holy God, Holy Mighty, Holy Immortal have mercy on us

I am taken back years to when I sang this same hymn in a darkened bedroom as my children's first lullaby. I chanted it softly as I rocked them to sleep. I chose it instinctively for its simplicity and its soothing repetitiveness. I never thought about how I was entwining for my children, at a most primal level, love and death. But I realize now that so much Orthodox practice does exactly this. We weave this strange paradox by countless small concrete acts of care and affection for the dead: the Psalms we read as they await burial, the candles we light when we pray for them, the painted eggs we leave at their tombstones when we sing, "Christ is Risen!" and picnic on their graves. And on Holy Friday, we tie the tapestry's first and final knot. After venerating the icon of Christ's broken body with kisses, we sing the most stunning hymns of the church year, the Lamentations, over Christ's tomb—a tomb we can barely see for all the flowers we have heaped upon it.

Think

From these and similar acts practiced without any sense of compulsion, our children learn that love is as strong as death, and in the end, it is stronger. I see it in my sons' faces as they bend to kiss Bob goodbye. I hear it in their laughter and reminiscences about Bob during the ride home.

Do not be afraid to hold your children close to the paradoxes of faith, even the painful ones. The mystery these paradoxes contain expands with life and death, with love and loss, with reality in all its complexity; they are the truths we do not outgrow. God ever hears our song. Love will win.

Pray

Holy God, Holy Mighty, Holy Immortal have
   mercy on us.
Holy God, Holy Mighty, Holy Immortal have
   mercy on us.
Holy God, Holy Mighty, Holy Immortal have
   mercy on us.

Act

Taking a walk in a cemetery together to enjoy the beauty
and fascinating details of the tombstones (especially if you
have a historic cemetery nearby) can be the first step in crack-
ing open the mystery of death with children. That people are
loved and yet lost to us for a time is a truly universal experience. All the different ways people grieve that loss, celebrate
that love, and, for some, wait in the hope of reunion are on
display in a cemetery and great fodder for conversation about
how we ourselves make meaning of it all.

Orthodox Christians mark the anniversary of a loved
one's death by making a ritual dish to be shared with the
community. The sweetness of that traditional dish is enjoyed
by all who loved the person while they share sweet memories
of them. You might try a similar and parallel practice of making and sharing the favorite dessert of someone you loved
who is no longer physically with you. Use the opportunity to
name some sweet memories of them.

Section V
Loosening Up

The next set of reflections invites us as caregivers to lean into the freedom and play of children. Sometimes our rules about how children should behave end up pulling them away from their authentic expressions of self. However, these authentic expressions are often learned for us as adults, and they can be opportunities to deepen and affirm the faith of children.

43

And a Child Shall Lead Them

JESSICA YOUNG BROWN

Read

I file into the quiet sanctuary with my two kids, aged two and seven. We are celebrating with a friend of mine who is transitioning to a new ministry placement. The style of worship at this church is very different than our own—pretty quiet and reserved in contrast to our livelier worship style. My seven-year-old son is able to read the room, but his little sister, the two-year-old COVID baby who I like to joke is "unchurched" because she has been to church so infrequently, only knows the more boisterous form of worship she has been exposed to and has decided to bring the energy with her! After the choir finishes a mellow selection, the congregation politely applauds. My daughter, who has been clapping and dancing the entire time, begins a rousing "Yeah! Wooohooo!" accompanied by hearty applause that I am certain can be heard in every inch of the sanctuary despite our discrete perch in the corner of the balcony. I am mortified. She is thrilled. The congregants are delighted and smiles abound. Later, after our friend offers a pastoral prayer, she yells, "Amen!" over and above the muted and dutiful refrain of the other parishioners.

"Thank you, Sasha, for being my amen corner," he remarks from the pulpit.

"You're welcome!" she yells. More chuckles from the congregation. More of me is wishing I could disintegrate into my pew. Despite all I know about childhood development, the playfulness of children, and what we say is the safety of the Christian community, I am now sitting with the shame of being a mother with a disruptive child. It nags at me despite my better judgment. But the longer I sit, the more I see the gift she has offered. Her participation in worship was more connected and attuned than many adults can muster through the busy noise in our minds and spirits. Her worship was contagious in a way that celebrated the offerings that others had brought to worship and invited all of us to settle down and really *be* together. Her actions encouraged us to do more than go through the motions but to really experience what was available to us in our moments of worship. She was paying attention and responsive to worship. And she was free! A model for us all.

Think

Many of us are familiar with Jesus' words in Mark 10:14: "Let the children come to me. Don't stop them! For the Kingdom of God belongs to those who are like these children" (NLT). But it would do us good to really think about what it means to engage the world and our faith with the curiosity, playfulness, and awe of children. Instead of molding children into the image of our adulthood, what would it look like to affirm children, their questions, and their ways of worship just as they are without revision or pruning? What can they teach us as we journey together in faith?

Pray

Loving and joyful God, help us to nurture and expand the playful parts of ourselves so that we always have an awe for you and your wonder. Help us to have the wisdom to be led by children whose connection with you is free and unfettered. Amen.

Act

Spend some time intentionally delighting in and affirming what your children bring to interactions with you and with others. Tell them things that you are learning from them in everyday life.

44

And I'm Way More!

TAMAR WASOIAN

Read

It was the field trip day at the daycare and the three-, four-, and five-year-old classes were so excited. But as a teacher, I hated field trips! They made me very anxious, and I was always on high alert. We filled the buses and headed to the zoo, and I made sure that several parent chaperones followed us in their cars. After visiting the lion, the monkeys, and all the other "sad friends because they were in cages," we walked to the bathrooms. The bathrooms were located in the same part of the building that hosted an experiential learning center about farming. Between back-and-forth bathroom trips, I realized that the youngest child was not with the group. My assistant and I ran around looking for him, and by the time I was back, he was sitting with his friends, enjoying his snack. He went to see the farmer's bright red truck. Who could blame his curiosity?

Later that day, as he was the last child to be picked up, I had time to talk with his mother. I shared with her the day's adventure. He was playing with his toys but paying attention to our conversation. At the end, I looked at him and said, "Man, you are something!"

He turned to me and simply said, "And I am way more!"

Think

Sometimes, we get caught up in our anxieties and fears, and we forget all the other wonderful things we experience during the day. Sometimes we forget how our children are made wonderfully and amazingly. We get focused on misbehaviors and forget to look behind them to see the amazing potential each child brings with them to this world. "And I am way more!" This child knew that he is a gift to us, that he is God's gift for us.

Pray

Open our eyes and minds to see all the blessings our children bring to us and to our society. Help us nurture them so that they also recognize their own gifts, and so they also appreciate how wonderfully you created us in your image.

Act

When your child breaks a rule, sit down with them and try to understand the reasons for their behavior and ours. How can we who care for children be more attentive to what is happening to the children we are watching? Are they motivated by curiosity, fear of some kind, or just absent-mindedness? This will teach us and them about their intentions and the impacts their actions might have. Also, be transparent about your own fears and anxieties and how you manage them. These are the best lessons you can teach your child.

45

When Mario Came to Church

DENISE JANSSEN

Read

I had a special connection with a seven-year-old in a congregation I served. He always brought action figures with him to church, and after he ran to me for his weekly hug, I made it a practice to ask him to introduce me to the action figures who came with him and tell me about their week. Luigi (from Mario Kart) typically came along to church, but one week it was Mario instead. After introductions, I told the child that he probably wanted to show Mario around and help him know how things worked at church.

The child thought that was a good idea and began telling Mario, "Here's the piano, and here's the place where the pastor talks, and here's the tall table where we sometimes have food but now there's a . . . Pastor Denise, what is that?" He was pointing to a pitcher and bowl we used for baptisms that sat symbolically on the table on weeks when Communion was not served. I explained the pitcher and bowl and how he was baptized when he was very small. We talked about how the church made promises to him, to his family, and to God to always make room for him and his needs in our congregation. We put a little water from my water bottle into the bowl, touched it with our hands, and put it on our heads. The child made sure Mario got some water on his head to remember his baptism. Then, he dipped Mario head-first and sloshed him around a little, just to be sure! After a few silent moments, he said to Mario, "This is the coolest place ever!" and was off to continue showing Mario around, teaching him how things worked around the church.

In that moment with this child, I learned again the importance of taking seriously the characters in children's lives as well as the impact of rituals and symbols. Far from being beyond his understanding, the opportunity to "teach" Mario about the church became a moment when this child could ask questions and try out the language of faith. Our experience that day taught me again the importance of taking seriously the children in our midst and their very real expressions of faith.

Think

Children's lives are filled with wonder as they strive to make sense of how the world works. They need the help of the grown-ups in their lives in this process. When a child wonders aloud or asks a question, it is an invitation to help them with categories and frameworks to make sense of their experiences. As important grown-ups in a child's life, we are invited to take seriously their wonderings and to help make connections with faith. When the child in this story "taught" his action figure, he was trying out some faith practices for himself, as well.

Pray

God of all, give me ears to hear beyond the words children say. Help me understand how to enter into their wondering to learn with them as they learn about you. Amen.

Act

Ask a child in your life to introduce an action figure or character from their play. We can learn so much through the characters that inhabit their play life and imagination. Share your wondering, even wondering about faith, as you talk together.

46

A Big Ask to Creatively Form Faith

AMY HOWARD

Read

Around the time my son turned seven, he began refusing to attend any children's ministry programming at our church. We could not figure out why, but it was clear he was not going to participate, no matter how we enticed him. This was especially complicated because I am a pastor. Around the same time, he also began refusing to attend school. Thankfully, the school administrator and guidance counselor sat down with me, and in a conversation filled with compassion, they came up with a plan to get him to school. The new plan gave him the responsibility of helping in one of the pre-K classes at the start of the school day. From that point on, going to school was a breeze even on the hard days because he did not want to miss out on helping.

When the summer came around and Vacation Bible School approached, I made a huge request to try at church what had worked at school. Our children's ministry team jumped on the idea. One of the parents who was volunteering in pre-K immediately agreed to have him as a "junior crew leader."

After almost a full year of refusing to participate in children's ministry, he instead had the week of his life, participating as fully as possible in it all. In every moment, he had a smile that stretched across his face as he proudly led the pre-K children around, helped them with crafts, cleaned up, and learned about Jesus' love as he leaned in, too. He was all-in and experienced a week of faith development that was just what his soul needed. It required out-of-the-box thinking and the openness of many adults leading children's ministry. As a result, it made a world of difference for him and for this mama.

Think

Every child learns differently, connects differently, and has unique challenges. Instead of accepting that children's ministry is one-size-fits-all, we are called to think creatively about how we establish an inclusive experience for all children. For any child who does not respond within the current norms, we need to meet them where they are. To adequately meet the needs of children today, there is a necessity for finding room to move beyond a rigid model for ministry.

Pray

God of koinonia, you are the one who has shown us how important community is. It gives us the support we need and helps us deepen our faith. We pray for wisdom for the caregivers who feel like there is no place for their children within the current community. Lead, guide, and direct them so all might be able to experience your love. Amen.

Act

In many of our churches, the creative thinking will have to come from you, parents/caregivers, who know your children best. Just as you are the primary advocate at school, so it is in your worshiping community. Do not be afraid to think creatively and make a big ask of the children's ministry team if it seems as though there is no place for the unique needs of your child. Their ability to experience God's love is just as important as the child beside them.

47

No More Diapers!

TAMAR WASOIAN

Read

A child named Casy (a fictitious name) in the preschool where I worked walked into the classroom and declared: no more diapers! Casy was almost three years old, but she knew exactly what she wanted all along. Her mother and I both knew Casy well, but we were not sure if her body was ready to catch up with her will.

I told Casy's mom that we would respect what Casy wanted. "Bring us more clothes so we can change them as frequently as necessary, and we will be okay," I assured her mother. We had many bathroom trips in the near future until her mind and body agreed with each other.

For the following few days, Casy ran to the bathroom anytime one of the other children needed to do so. We did have a few accidents, but we didn't focus on them much. Instead, we celebrated all the right timings and true alarms.

Although we compromised on nap-time pull-ups, Casy was fine with that because pull-ups were like underwear, you know, and she could put them on by herself. In a few days, we no longer needed those frequent runs, and Casy did not need any diapers or changes anymore.

Think

In Deuteronomy 32:11, God's providential care to Israel is painted "as an eagle stirs up its nest and hovers over its young; as it spreads its wings, takes them up, and bears them aloft on its pinions."

Very often, parents and caregivers behave as eagles hovering over to protect their children. Adults assume that such care is necessary for children's survival, and that is quite true for infants and toddlers. But as children grow, parents and caring adults need to learn when to step back and let their children practice independence and have a sense of their own agency. Toilet training is such an important developmental milestone for children. I have seen them emerge triumphantly as strong, independent little persons, even sometimes with the subtle arrogance of a "now I can do it all by myself!" attitude. I witnessed the free will emerging so subtly and so wonderfully in the children of this stage. Respecting children's will is fundamentally important for building their own assertive selves, even if sometimes they are not exactly equipped with the physical, emotional, or intellectual abilities needed for success. Being supportive sometimes means frequent runs to the bathroom, and dealing with soiled clothes and wet shoes. It reminds me of how much mess God has patiently dealt with in parenting humankind for all this time!

Pray

As you watch over us like a caring eagle, help us learn from you how to care for and support the little persons you entrust to our care. Teach us how to hover gracefully and let them go when they need to spread their own wings, and grant us the wisdom to know the difference.

Act

An educator's advice: Never ever have a confrontation with a child. They will always win. Shift the scenario to a conversation where there are no losers or winners.

48

Calming Spaces

LUCAS PEPPER

Read

My primary calling as an ordained United Methodist Deacon is to serve as a bridge between the church and the world. I began my diaconal ministry serving within an affluent, suburban congregation where I helped to guide youth and adults as they learned to grow as agents of change in the world and how to discern and meet the diverse needs of everyone within the local community and beyond.

I now serve as a special education teacher in a public middle school in the suburbs of Chicago. As a part of my job for the past couple of years, I have been blessed to co-teach a class period designed for students who struggle with social norms and communication skills. The class begins with quiet time, where students may choose a quiet activity while calming music plays so they can regulate. I had a student who loved to spend that time making little creations, from paper airplanes to fortresses made of kinetic sand. This student struggled with communication about anything that did not fascinate him, and often, it was difficult to tell if any of our lessons were ever getting through. One day during quiet time, I was walking around the room, and when I came near him, he said quite plainly but confidently, "You know why I like this class?" Before I could respond, he said, "Because it is so calm and relaxing to be in this room." That class period became a sense of calm for him in a busy, demanding middle-school day. The primary goal was for him to become successful at social communication, but his need for being calm and centered needed to be met first.

Think

A belief that those we support have needs and require space to just be and to be accepted for who they are is central to my ministry. Everyone has talents, gifts, and beautiful characteristics that make up who they are and need to be honored. The work of affirmation and care for individuals, no matter how young or old, does not come without its challenges. How are you providing space so that children in your life have space to be who they are and to share their gifts and talents? We all could use that same time each day to be calm and to center ourselves. When I have been at my best in my ministry, it is because I first cared for my well-being, surrounded myself with those who cared for and supported me, and at the same time, set clear boundaries to ensure that I was not overextending myself. Where and how do you find a calm and relaxing space to center yourself?

Pray

Loving and gracious God, as I serve as a caring bridge for others in my life, I pause to give you thanks for the ways you have been a foundation for me and cared for me on my journey. May your spirit guide me as I seek to affirm and support others for who you created them to be. Amen.

Act

Provide a calm and relaxing space for your children to unwind from their day. This may be a ritual of nightly prayer, listening to music together, or some other way to provide a sense of calm in a busy day.

49

Being Heard Is Being Loved

SHELLEY WILLMANN WEAKLY

Read

"Mommy, I know how God grows!" exclaimed my five-year-old son. We were standing in front of a tiny grave in our backyard where we had just buried our beloved pet rabbit, Benjamin Bunny. "When someone dies and goes to be with God, they make God bigger." He had been in tears just a moment ago, and this was obviously not the time for a theological discussion on whether animals have souls and go to heaven. It was a time to listen.

When my sons were young, they freely shared their thoughts, feelings, and insights. I discovered that it was important to listen to the least little thing because it was impossible to tell where their words might lead. As the boys grew older and were influenced by our culture to think that it was not cool to talk about their feelings and hopes, sometimes they needed a little encouragement. One activity our family tried was having "caring conversations" around the dinner table involving questions such as, "If you could have any superpower you wanted, what would it be?" Then we would discuss the answers. This gave them the opportunity to engage in conversation in a non-threatening environment, which ensured that their answers would be heard and not ridiculed. We could then move on to deeper questions like, "How could you use that superpower for God?"

Sometimes my children had questions about God. I discovered that it was not as important for me to have the correct answers as to listen for the meaning behind the question and encourage them to keep asking. One time, my younger son, aged seven, was talking about a problem at school, and I suggested we pray about it. He responded, "Praying doesn't work." As I listened to his disappointment instead of being horrified by this statement, we were able to have a good discussion about prayer.

Think

All people need to experience being listened to and heard. Currently, a meme with a quotation by David W. Augsburger is circulating around social media, which states, "Being heard is so close to being loved that for the average person, they are almost indistinguishable." In my work as a chaplain, I have experienced this over and over again. Listening deeply and truly hearing another person demonstrates respect and care. These practices forge strong bonds and build trust. If we listen to children when they share little things with us, they know that we will be available when they have bigger problems to discuss. In addition, by giving them a sense of being heard, we help them to understand that God always hears us.

Pray

Listening God, help me to silence my inner distractions so that I can truly hear my children. Help me to be available for them, just as you are always available for us.

Act

Have a caring conversation with your child. Ask something like, "If you could solve any problem in the world, what would it be?" Discuss their answer, listening for the feelings behind the response. Then pray about how together you can make a difference.

50

Curating Curiosity

PAULA CRIPPS-VALLEJO

Read

I was having backyard summer fun with my five-year-old and, in the midst of the energy and joy, he stopped, looked, and said, "So, God is like everywhere, but also, I cannot see God, right? And God is like in my heart but also in that butterfly and tree? Cool. But, how? Also, what does God look like and why can't we see God?"

Wow! I have a Master of Divinity, and I have been a pastor for more than fifteen years, but as a parent, I am still sometimes unsure about to answer our kids' big and important questions. How do we explain why when we do not feel like we understand?

I found myself saying, "Those are such good questions, my little love. I don't know exactly how or why, but I do believe that God is everywhere in the whole big universe. And that we can see God in each other's eyes. In the squirrel running up on that tree. And we hear God in the birds chirping. And the cicadas who come out at night."

And he replied, "That's true. All of that. And in so many other places. I especially love that God is in my heart. And in your heart. And we hear God's voice when we say 'I love you' to each other. I love you, Mama. Let's play freeze tag!"

Think

An important part of our faith is embracing the mystery of God, who is both as close as a friend and beyond our understanding. As parents and caregivers, we can help our children embrace the mystery of God by wondering with them, sharing questions together, and being okay with not having all the answers.

Pray

God, who is everywhere in the universe and in our hearts, we thank you for welcoming our questions and are glad to find you in all the hows and whys. Help us to see you in each other and in the beauty of your creation and guide our spirits to play with the Holy Spirit each day!

Act

When do we stop being so curious? How do we make sure our limited grown-up views do not hamper the faith of the children? We ask them questions. We answer their questions. We show them through our actions that we are open to the movement of the Holy Spirit. We teach them through our faith that questions are not the opposite of faith but the core of our faith. We use our voices to say, "I love you, and God loves you." And we play freeze tag!

Find a way today to enter into the curiosity of a child. And maybe even play a game of freeze tag!

51

A Dollar that Brings My Family Together

JENNA WILLIAMS

Read

We are not regular churchgoers, but we go on holidays such as Christmas and Easter. The Christmas children's mass with a pageant is always a favorite for my entire family. When I was a kid, my mom would always give all the kids one dollar to put in the basket during the offering. This tradition carried well into adulthood for us. There would be three grown adults squished in a pew, reaching toward the older lady on the end for a single dollar each. We would spend a few minutes folding the dollar into different shapes and objects before the offering came by for us to put it in. We were fully aware of the weird looks we got from those around us, but we were not bothered.

As grandchildren came along, my mom made sure she had enough dollars for her adult children and grandchildren. Sometimes, my mom would call and ask who was going to church because "she wanted to make sure she had enough dollars." It was never about the dollars or even if we went to church, but it was more about coming together as a family.

She wanted to make sure we were going to have our once-a-year time when we were all together as a large family. With three kids living in different areas, each with busy schedules and kids of their own, it was always about taking a pause from life and making a point of unifying and being together. The holidays, particularly Christmas, are about that. While we would not be considered a very religious family, practicing our faith brings us together as a family and support network. When we gather for the holidays once a year, it is a reminder we have each other. We may be physically apart for much of the year, but our common bond through our faith helps make sure we take time to come together.

My mom could not attend church this year, but as the time in the service approached for the offerings, my oldest son leaned over and asked if someone still brought the dollars since grandma was not there. Almost in unison, my siblings and I pulled out dollars for each person sitting in the pew. While we were passing out the dollars, my brother who lives the farthest away leans to me and said, "Regardless of what happens, I'm always going to try to make it here."

Think

Like so many aspects of parenting, I question whether I am doing a good job of building my children's religious education and faith. The moment my son asked for his dollar to put in the offering helped me recognize my children are beginning to recognize the importance of how faith brings us together. Each individual may have their unique relationship and approach to faith, but one hope I have is for my children to learn and recognize the power of how faith can bring people together.

Pray

God, who makes big things happen from just a little, thank you for taking the simple offering of our dollars and using it to bring our family together in faith. Amen.

Act

Whether as part of worship or just during daily life, take an opportunity today to reflect on those actions you take that model for the children you care for a value or faith practice that is important to you. Take that action today. Intentionality matters!

52

Wondering Together

MELANIE BLACK

Read

"What's gravity?"

"I wonder if the rabbits in the yard are married?"

These are the types of queries my daughter has when the lights go out, and she is supposed to be falling asleep. One night when she was three years old, she said something like, "God made everything." Then she started talking about things she had heard at church when she visited with my mother-in-law. And I froze up. My husband and I grew up in Christian churches, but we left organized religion in college. For me it felt too literal, too dogmatic at best, and occasionally hypocritical at worst. I tried my best to stay curious and open with my daughter. I asked her what she had learned and what she thought about it. I want her to have opportunities to be part of a spiritual community, to explore things bigger than us with wonder and awe, to know the power and sacredness of love, and to practice living meaningful values. But honestly, I did not know what that would look like for us.

I know she will be exposed to spiritual and religious topics within our extended family and culture. Instead of shutting those experiences down, I want to help give context and depth to the things she hears and sees. This bedtime conversation made me begin to imagine what her spiritual education could be. Instead of running away from the discomfort, I leaned into it and I admitted that I did not have all the answers. We talk about Jesus as a very kind and important teacher. We read books about lessons from sacred texts in world religions or about the connectedness of all people, animals, and the earth. We look for times when love, nature, and music feel like real magic. I went out and found a spiritual community in an unstructured Quaker meeting that aligns with my beliefs, and we are finding new ways to explore faith and spirit.

"What do you think God is like?" I asked her at bedtime recently.

She thought about it. "I think God is like a person but magical. I think God might have been the first person."

"That's a cool idea," I said, and we had a really nice conversation about what and who and where we thought God is before she drifted off to sleep.

Think

Children are capable of understanding and exploring complex topics. They can be creative and thoughtful and deserve to be treated with respect. It is more valuable to me to teach my daughter to think and explore for herself rather than to memorize and obey without question.

Pray

May we have the courage to accept uncertainty and be vulnerable with our children. May we give them permission and agency to explore faith and spiritual life. And may we joyfully cultivate their curiosity with our own curiosity, accepting and enjoying the beautiful mystery of life together.

Act

Be curious about your child's inner world. Share your beliefs about faith, but do so with vulnerability and openness, admitting that you do not have all the answers. Invite your child to explore their own beliefs. You could preface the conversation with something like, "God means a lot of different things to different people. What does God mean to you?" Ask them what they think God is. What does God look like? Where is God? When is God? If your child thinks God is "magical," ask them when have they felt or seen real magic.

Conclusion

Now I lay me down to sleep,
I pray the Lord my Soul to keep.
If I should die before I wake,
I pray the Lord my Soul to take.

For a long time, this bedtime prayer seemed to be universal. There was also a time when public school mornings began with prayer and even songs about Jesus. It was a time when church, family, and school intersected. It was not necessarily better, but it was the reality at the time. Traditionally, especially in certain regions of the United States, prayer was a major staple of life.

This is not an effort to spiritualize the past but an effort to draw special attention to the habits and practices of those who attend church. We are not advocates who believe our past traditions were so sanctimonious that we need to live in a world of nostalgia, making statements like, "Those were the good old days." However, there is something powerful to be said about tradition and its importance in the lives of those who nurture faith. The Cambridge Dictionary defines tradition in this way: "a belief, principle, or way of acting that people in a particular society or group have continued to follow for a long time, or all of these beliefs in a particular society or group."[1] Tradition is more than just passing on information or beliefs; it is a connection to the past and our ancestors. Tradition means something different to everyone, but it is important and should be preserved. For some people, tradition means following religious rituals or celebrating cultural holidays. For others, it may mean cooking the same recipe for Thanksgiving every year or wearing the same dress to their brothers' weddings. Whatever it may be, tradition is special and important. It is not always easy to keep traditions alive, but it is worth trying. Sometimes it only takes one person to start carrying on the tradition, and then it can spread to the rest of the family or community. Preserving traditions is key when it comes to things like passing down stories or old recipes to keep our history alive.

Tradition is also an important part of identity. It connects us to our roots and helps us understand our origins. It can be a source of comfort in difficult times, reminding us of who we are and what we stand for. As we reflect on what it means to raise faithful kids, we understand that our familial, cultural, and religious traditions can be a vital piece of this puzzle. However, as many of our contributors name in various ways, our families change, the circumstances of our lives change, and we often face a lack of ability or desire to pass on traditions as we once did. So, we ask ourselves, how do we pass down tradition when the thing we did in the past no longer works?

In this moment, we are challenged to re-tradition. The life of the Johnsons illustrates how this might take place. Prior to the untimely death of Cortez Johnson's wife, Joan, they had hosted a Thanksgiving dinner for both sides of their family for more than thirty years. After Joan's death, Cortez continued this tradition, but the family-favorite macaroni and cheese was missing because there was no replacement for Joan's culinary expertise with that dish. Nevertheless, the tradition continued each Thanksgiving Day for nine years after Joan's death. Two major events changed the trajectory of the long-time tradition: Cortez remarried, and a global pandemic made family gatherings impossible.

Cortez now had a new set of in-laws who lived easily within driving distance from the Johnsons' newly established home. Two traditions collided. Helen, the new wife, had her own well-established practice of spending Thanksgiving Day with her mother. This tradition included taking her mother shopping and helping with the cooking.

What was once Cortez's home alone for nine years had now become Cortez and Helen's home. What once was a home hosting up to forty people that Cortez had known for decades had now become an empty house on Thanksgiving Day. Cortez and his immediate family were forced to adapt and re-tradition their Thanksgiving. The blending of the families forced them to find a new way to honor what was important.

Life changes. So do traditions, even when we are not ready—especially when we are not ready. Having to re-tradition is not so much about finding new traditions; it is about taking treasured traditions, remembering their purpose, and finding ways to keep those purposes alive. Everyone tweaks holiday traditions: we find better recipes, include someone new on the guest list, or maybe update the linens used at the family meal. When the family matriarch can no longer host the gathering because she has moved from her long-time home, other family members pick up the mantle and open their homes.

To re-tradition is about something bigger than changing direction and doing new things. It involves defining the tradition, understanding its importance, and naming its purpose. This process helps us to return to the core of what matters while we manage an ever-changing life.

For the Johnson family, the tradition was defined as keeping and engaging the legacy left to them by their ancestors—a legacy of love and care for one another through intentional fellowship. If Cortez's immediate family had allowed anything but love to abound, it probably would have led to anger and resentment. However, because of the love and care for one another in the immediate family, they understood why the

Thanksgiving Day gathering had to desist from its past habits so that Cortez could participate in his new wife's tradition. The process of re-traditioning for the Johnson family created new spaces for family gatherings. It was not without its challenges, but it was successful. Cortez's new wife and his immediate family began to gather on other occasions and continue the tradition of family fellowship.

How does this story about Thanksgiving Day dinner relate to a bedtime prayer? Well, the case we are making is that this bedtime prayer became popular because of the pedagogical method referred to as "banking" or the transmission model. It describes the method where the teacher is the sole expert, pouring all the information into students who become the object of the knowledge.[2]

The bedtime story is banking in that children for decades have memorized it with the thought that it was shaping their faith. It was a nice ritual, but formation was not happening. It was a simple transmission of knowledge. It was a nice tradition, but the true formation of children might require a re-traditioning of the ritual to assist children in their being nurtured into the faith. This is not a proposal to abandon the bedtime prayer, but an invitation to assist the prayer to become R.E.A.L. (Relational, Experiential, Applicable, and Lifelong) in the lives of those who practice this ritual.[3]

We want to emphasize that the point is not to abandon the tradition but to re-tradition the rituals we have lived with by finding ways to build **Relationships** and ways to open the hearts and minds of children to deeper meanings of the prayer by going beyond repeating the prayer each night. As many of our contributors have affirmed, our faith formation practice requires that we be in consistent, meaningful relationships with the kids we love and care for. We need to be with them, work to understand them, and listen to them.

The way toward receiving deeper meanings of ritual is by helping children to **Experience** the core of their importance. This might be done through a game or activity completed before bedtime. It could also be done by engaging the senses, as many contributors have suggested. A key component of this is also attending to our emotional experiences to connect. By providing an experience for children to be actively involved, an emotional reaction is more likely to be evoked and learning can be deepened.

Applying what kids are learning to their daily lives is another component of helping children unlock their faith. Pumping kids' brains full of facts and data will not lead to life changes. Leading kids into a deeper relationship with God happens through transformation, not information. As so many of our contributors offer, this means we always take time to dig into and address questions, no matter how big or small. Curiosity is a pathway to meaningful application.

While the original acronym employed the word "Learn" for its last letter, we choose to use the word **Lifelong**. Although parents have done a great job of helping children memorize the words of the bedtime prayer and other routines, those actions have not necessarily propelled children to a lifelong relationship with God. It is our contention that the bedtime prayer, for example, is based on a schooling model of education where memorizing and reciting information is encouraged. Re-traditioning involves going deeper and beginning a process that will cause children to take ownership and build an intrinsic desire to learn and grow in their faith.

Several of the reflections in this volume point us to re-tradition things such as prayer, storytelling, and memorization of Scripture. There are many opportunities for this. We may hear people refer to doing things as "out of the box" or "doing a new thing." Those nuances could also be labeled as finding a way to re-tradition.

We also want to invite you to re-tradition another thing: your role in the lives of the kids you love. Whether you are a parent, grandparent, godparent, foster parent, aunt, uncle, teacher, or another safe adult, we encourage you to think about faith formation as a part of your caring role. Every interaction is an opportunity to teach, and teaching is bigger and broader than the words you say. Sometimes we are required to shift the way we think, the rules we follow, and the values that guide our behavior and our interactions in order to re-tradition.

Re-Tradition Our Self-Understandings—Caregivers and Parents as Primary in Faith Formation

When Virginia was serving a United Methodist church in the 1990s as a Christian educator for age-level ministries, one of the highlights of the summer was a youth mission trip to Hinton Rural Life Center in the southwestern part of North Carolina. Their summer program involved repairing homes and building new homes. It was the trip that most youth wanted to attend, and the church helped to make that possible.

She remembers one conversation with several members about who should be allowed to participate with some persons wanting a "church attendance quota" for youth to register for the event. They thought that youth who did not participate in church events as often as others should not be allowed to attend. In response, Virginia did some calculations. Sunday school classes at that church were supposed to be approximately sixty minutes, but the reality was that they were forty-five-minute sessions since they were often late starting for a variety of reasons. If a youth attended Sunday School every week of the year, they were a part of a Christian education experience for about thirty-nine hours of the year. When youth attended the summer mission trip, they were with adult counselors for approximately sixty-six hours. (Eighteen-hour round trip in a van traveling to and from the Center, and at least twelve hours a day—meals, work, devotions, etc.— for four days = forty-eight hours.)

So, Virginia made two points in her conversation with those members: (1) youth who did not attend church regularly would get more Christian education opportunities on the trip than they would in an entire year of Sunday school; (2) many of those youths were in situations that would not allow them to attend every Sunday (family living situations, school events, etc.). The congregation certainly should not penalize students for something that was not their fault.

But the main reason for encouraging participation was because Virginia knew that teenagers would ask her and other adult counselors questions on a trip that they would not ask at church. They asked questions while they were riding in the van to the Center. They asked questions while hammering shingles on a roof on a ninety-five-degree day. They asked questions while sitting in rocking chairs on the front porch of the Center at the end of the day. And they asked questions sitting around the breakfast or dinner table and at many other places—all outside of a classroom. Their questions were important, dealing with a variety of situations and experiences. Often, their questions were opportunities for them to explore potential answers with people they had come to know and trust because those adults and mentors had chosen to spend a week of vacation on this trip.

This experience happened in the first few years of Virginia's ministry after graduating from seminary. One of her religious education professors, Dr. John Westerhoff, had been questioning and critiquing the schooling model of Christian education for some time.[4] As referenced above, religious education has often followed the secular model and trends of education. Some trends were helpful for Christian education, like the use of current technology to provide or illustrate information. New research in psychology and education provided information about how children grow and develop that was helpful not only to public school systems but to church education as well. But some of those educational advances were better suited to a different context than our present time.

The landscape of religious education and faith formation has changed drastically in the last decade. A pandemic and declining church participation has created opportunities to re-imagine (or re-tradition) what faith formation might look like.

Re-Tradition Education and Caregiver's Role

When hearing the word *education*, one often envisions schools with classrooms and teachers. When hearing the term religious education, one often envisions another kind of school with classrooms and teachers—Sunday school. Sunday schools have been a consistent feature of some denominations and faith traditions for over two hundred years. Other models were available, but the "schooling model" became prevalent. We suggest drawing upon some of the possibilities of educational roads not taken when thinking of ways to re-tradition Christian education.

Sophia Lyon Fahs and Nelle Morton, twentieth century religious educators, spoke to the ideas of collaboration, agency, and mutuality in education and learning. In 1939, Fahs wrote about child-centered education, collaborative learning, and the partnership between the teacher and the student: "The teacher was to be someone who led the children to experiences of wonder, rather than someone who gave answers or transmitted cognitive knowledge. The teacher was to be someone who assisted in finding ways for the child to have direct experiences in finding out something for themselves . . . [Fahs] gave great weight to the agency of the child."[5]

Morton believed that God's grace was present in moments of deep listening, and that equality and mutuality were foundational for religious education. Writing in 1960, Morton said:

> The communal nature of the church itself includes both the
> adult and the child in a mutual ministry which the Word
> brought into being and to which the Word speaks. There-
> fore, listening becomes as important for the adult's becom-
> ing as for the child's. Listening to a child may be a means

by which God's grace and judgment impart themselves to self-sufficient and pride-prone teachers and parents. It may involve being delivered from exalted self-images and entering the very life of the other.[6]

The word *education* comes from the Latin root word *educare*, which means "to lead or to draw out." Contrary to some popular opinions, it does not mean to "pour into." Yes, there is content that one learns, but to educate means to help someone develop and understand who they are and what gifts they have to offer their community. This is exactly what happened with the youth who participated in the summer mission experience described previously. They were better able to explore their own identity and gifts through questions and conversations one-on-one with caring adults. You, as a caregiver who spends big and small moments with kids, also have the opportunity to help them develop and understand themselves and their faith as you navigate life together.

The concepts of explicit, implicit, and null curriculum may be helpful as we consider how to teach and educate. Curriculum means "the course to be run," and it includes the materials used in a learning situation, the blueprint or plan for learning, and how everything in the learning environment teaches. The explicit curriculum is what we list, print, or say that we are teaching. The implicit curriculum is what we may be unaware that we are teaching, maybe by one's language, by who is allowed to participate, and so on. (It is also known as the hidden curriculum.) The null curriculum is what is taught by what is excluded or left out.

The pandemic provided an opportunity for religious educators to recognize several important drawbacks of the current model of faith formation:

- A schooling model of education, whether in the church or public school, is not easily adapted.

- Educators who relied on the physical presence of children to teach found it hard to imagine alternate ways of teaching.

- Educators felt disconnected from the needs of children and parents or caregivers; in-person teaching gave educators ways to connect and communicate with children. During the pandemic other ways of communicating were needed.

- It was hard for many to adapt to technology due to a lack of access, resources, or training.

- Parents and caregivers found they needed more Christian education resources from their faith communities than were provided.[7]

Rather than a hasty return to pre-COVID models of faith formation, we invite you to reimagine (re-tradition) what Christian education and faith formation look like in the current context. Might that model be one where the home is the primary place of religious education, with parents and caregivers as a child's first teacher and pastor? The home would not be the only place of religious learning because religious education would be seen as a shared, collaborative effort between the family and the congregation. As many contributors have suggested, *raising faithful kids* is also about finding ways caregivers and faith communities can partner to equip children for a full and faithful life.

In his book *Lifelong Faith*, John Roberto notes that recent research confirms the role and centrality of parents, caregivers, and family in children's faith formation.[8] He notes four primary findings from the research:

1. The most significant influences on the faith formation of children come from parents or caregivers and their families.

2. Parents and caregivers model their faith through day-to-day practices within the family.

3. Those practices are nurtured within that family.[9]

4. The relationship between parent/caregiver and child, and the parenting practices, makes a significant difference, or as Roberto notes, *"How* parents and their children interact about religion has more influence on the outcome than the particular substance of what parents communicate."[10]

As noted in the opening chapter, Christian Smith and Amy Adamczyk's research in *Handing Down the Faith: How Parents Pass on Their Religion to the Next Generation* found that parents are their children's primary religious educators and home is the primary context. This is the case even when the congregation and Sunday school play a role; the parent/caregiver role is still primary. Just as Roberto found in his research, Smith and Adamczyk also found that emotional warmth and good communication from the parents make their teaching more effective. They found that talking with children about faith was the most important factor in effective faith formation.[11] This research can often sound like it is a one-way street, even if that is not what is intended.

Children are not blank slates ready to be programmed. Children are created in the image of God, and each child has unique gifts and talents. Children are born into their full humanity. That is not something that happens when they reach adulthood; it is happening all the time, and everywhere. They are important parts of their family and community. Helping children understand their roles in family and community ultimately helps them to understand who they are in the community of faith.

While some make the claim that children are the church of tomorrow, we, the authors, claim that children are the church today! They are moral persons with agency capable of creating change.[12] Rev. Dr. Karen Marie Yust, Director of the Children's Spirituality Hub at Union Presbyterian Seminary, describes how children can be collaborators in faith formation. Yust notes:

> Responsibility for children's religious education needs to take seriously children's agency and active participation. Children can and will flourish spiritually when encouraged to raise questions, explore diverse ideas and practices, and develop their own interpretations of what they see and hear. They can be trusted as collaborators in their own religious identity formation.[13]

Children are theologians. How can we journey with children as they make meaning and learn to live as faithful people in a world of multiple pandemics? As the Rev. Dr. Tanya Eustace Campen reminds us in her book *Holy Work Together: Making Meaning Together*:

> Recognizing that we journey together shifts the pedagogical paradigm. No longer are we the knowledge carriers, depositing information into the young empty minds of the children in our community. Instead, we become models of the faith as we demonstrate what it looks like to wonder, to articulate our reflections, and to practice living out our faith in a chaotic world. Adults who journey with children as shepherds and guides encourage and show them how to make meaning in response to God's presence (and perceived absence) in their lives. In this journey or dance to make meaning together, we recognize that every person, no matter their age, has an opportunity to live as a theologian. Our role is to encourage and support this calling. Children, then, are theologians too, making meaning out of stories and their experiences of God. We do this holy work together.[14]

Other research gives us information about practices that are important in faith formation. These include:

- Modeling: Young children need to see their parents or caregivers engaged in faith practices like Bible study, prayer, and attending church.

- Discussion: Parents need to provide opportunities for discussion about religious topics where children can listen and ask questions and give their own responses.

- Imagination: In hearing Bible stories, children should be encouraged to use their imagination through music, art, and movement.

This book's reflections testify to this research and provide you with practical examples of how to use this research to deepen your family's faith life and empower your children to own it.

These principles and practices of collaboration, agency, and mutuality have not changed, but the world in which we practice them has. We need to reimagine ways to practice what we consider important. We believe that this book is a step in reimagining new ways to practice our faith together.

In educational psychology, we talk about a concept called *craft knowledge*.[15] It is the awareness that, even in the evidence of rules, policies, and procedures, the people who are often most effective in their roles are able to do this because of intuition and wisdom that flows from their experience, the relationships they build, and their own sense of who they are. In this volume, we have invited parents, caregivers, and teachers to share their craft knowledge with you. Now, we as trained educators acknowledge that you know more than we do about your children. We invite you to take full responsibility for your role as a religious educator and to re-tradition how you imagine your role in the faith formation of the children you love and nurture. We invite you to use your own craft knowledge to support your shepherding of the children you love, recognizing that you have everything you need. We hope that these reflections will support you on this holy journey.

Notes

1. *Cambridge Dictionary Online*, s.v. "tradition," accessed September 5, 2023, https://dictionary.cambridge.org/us/dictionary/english/tradition.

2. To learn more about what the author means about the banking and transmission model see an explanation in *The Formation of a People*, Carmichael D. Crutchfield, 125.

3. The acronym R.E.A.L. is the philosophy that sets the tone for all of Group Ministries, Inc. curriculum. https://www.group.com/search-results/?q=real.

4. John H. Westerhoff, III, *Will Our Children Have Faith* (Toronto: Morehouse Publishing, 2000, Revised Edition).

5. Barbara Anne Keely, *Faith of Our Foremothers: Women Changing Religious Education* (Louisville: Westminster John Knox Press, 1997), 25.

6. Ibid., 47.

7. Fall 2022 Religious Educators Association Fall Meeting, panel discussion.

8. John Roberto, *Lifelong Faith: Formation for All Ages and Generations* (New York: Church Publishing, 2022), 60.

9. Ibid., 60–62.

10. Ibid., 63.

11. Christian Smith and Amy Adamczyk. *Handing Down the Faith: How Parents Pass Their Religion on to the Next Generation* (New York: Oxford University Press, 2021).

12. See Kate Ott works in bibliography for more on children as moral persons with agency; see Virginia A. Lee on children who are capable of creating change.

13. Karen-Marie Yust, "Whose Children are They? Talking about Responsibility for Children's Religious Education," Religious Education, 118:2, (2023): 87–93, DOI: 10.1080/00344087.2023.2198819.

14. Tanya Marie Eustace Campen, *Holy Work with Children: Making Meaning Together* (Eugene, Oregon: Pickwick Publications, 2021), 17.

15. Jan H. Van Driel, Nico Verloop, H. Inge Van Werven, and Hetty Dekkers. "Teachers' Craft Knowledge and Curriculum Innovation in Higher Engineering Education," Higher Education 34, no. 1 (1997): 105–122. https://doi.org/10.1023/A:1003063317210.

Bibliography

Campen, Tanya Marie Eustace. *Holy Work with Children: Making Meaning Together*. Eugene, Oregon: Pickwick Publications, 2021.

Crutchfield, Carmichael D. *Formation of A People: Christian Education in the African American Church*, Judson Press, 2020.

Keely, Barbara Anne. *Faith of Our Foremothers: Women Changing Religious Education*. Louisville: Westminster John Knox Press, 1997.

Lee, Virginia A. "Something Inside So Strong: Learning from the Freedom School Movement." In *Let Your Light Shine: Mobilizing for Justice with Children and Youth,* edited by Reginald Blount and Virginia A. Lee, 87–97. Washington, DC: Friendship Press, 2019.

Ott, Kate. "Ecclesiology of 'Do no stop them': Children, Creativity and Connection." In *Ecclesiology for a Digital Church*, edited by Heidi A. Campbell and John Dyer, 142–154. London: SCM Press, 2022.

Ott, Kate. "Taking Children's Moral Lives Seriously: Creativity as Ethical Response Offline and Online," *Religions* 2019, 10, 525; doi:10.3390/rel10090525.

Roberto, John. *Lifelong Faith: Formation for All Ages and Generations*. New York: Church Publishing, 2022.

Smith, Christian, and Amy Adamczyk. *Handing Down the Faith: How Parents Pass Their Religion on to the Next Generation*. New York: Oxford University Press, 2021.

Van Niekerk, M. & Breed, G., 2018, "The role of parents in the development of faith from birth to seven years of age," *HTS Teologiese Studies/Theological Studies* 74(2), a4773. https://doi.org/ 10.4102/hts.v74i2.4773.

Van Driel, Jan H., Nico Verloop, H., Inge Van Werven, and Hetty Dekkers. "Teachers' Craft Knowledge and Curriculum Innovation in Higher Engineering Education." *Higher Education* 34, no. 1 (1997): 105–122. https://doi.org/10.1023/A:1003063317210.

Westerhoff, III, John H. *Will Our Children Have Faith?* Toronto: Morehouse Publishing, 2000, Revised Edition.

Yust, Karen-Marie. (2023) "Whose Children are They? Talking about Responsibility for Children's Religious Education." *Religious Education*, 118:2, 87–93, DOI: 10.1080/00344087.2023.2198819.

Biographical Snapshots of the Contributors of Reflections in This Book

Toccoro A. Arrington is a newly licensed minister who has a passion to serve others by helping them experience the transforming power of prayer and faith. Her faith is rooted in a strong biblical foundation that was planted at a very early age in her life. She is often dedicated and motivated to help young people in their faith formation by the words echoed in James 2:26, "Just as the body without the spirit is dead, faith without works is also dead."

Rev. Ashley Prescott Barlow-Thompson (she/her) is an ordained deacon in the United Methodist Church serving as the Director of Christian Education and Justice Ministries at her church in Wichita, Kansas. Along with her work in the local church, she is passionate about being a good neighbor, friend, and parent! Outside of church and community work, Ashley can be found building Legos with her middle schooler, Prescott, playing folk music with her spouse, Adam, and finding joy in little things like iced tea, lunch out, holographic stickers, and a good book!

Melanie Black attended the University of Richmond undergraduate program and the College of William and Mary for graduate school. She is a part-time Licensed Professional Counselor and stay-at-home mom to a busy five-year-old. Melanie loves learning new things, watching sunsets, absorbing art in all forms, crafting, and participating in impromptu kitchen dance parties.

Dr. Keosha Branch is a Licensed Professional Counselor in the Commonwealth of Virginia and maintains a private practice in the city of Richmond. When she is not working with clients, she's spending time with her husband and three children. Dr. Branch also enjoys reading and writing in her spare time.

Nicole Brocato is a self-defined "student of life," who is always learning and observing the world around her. She loves a good cup of coffee, a great book, and thoughtful conversation. Brocato currently resides in the suburbs of Chicago with her husband, Anthony, and their two kids, Rowan and Amelia.

Emily Bryant, PhD, is a recovering perfectionist who often has stains on her clothes and is looking to laugh and grow with others. She is a Licensed Clinical Psychologist specializing in anxiety disorders. She lives in Richmond, Virginia, with her husband and two children.

Rev. Randy Creath has been journeying the path of music and theology his whole life. Pastoring churches, playing and writing Christian rock music, being an internet influencer, and romancing his wife are the daily joys of this father of two.

Rev. Paula Cripps-Vallejo is a United Methodist clergywoman who finds her calling at the intersections of prophetic and pastoral ministry. She currently serves as pastora at Humboldt Park UMC, a predominantly Latinx congregation in Chicago, and as Director of Resource Development at the Center for Changing Lives. Her deepest joy is in her family and finding hope with her spouse, two kids, and dog.

Dr. Carmichael D. Crutchfield is the Professor of Christian Education, Spiritual Formation and Youth Ministry at Memphis Theological Seminary. He also serves as the General Secretary of the Department of Christian Education and Formation of the Christian Methodist Episcopal Church.

Cindy A. Cummins knew as a child that one of her only goals in life was to be a mom to someone. God gave her two girls from China who fulfilled that dream. It is the hardest yet best job she has ever had.

Zanique Davis is a wife to her soulmate, Zamar, and a dynamic mother to her amazing boys, Zayn and Zayd. She is an ordained itinerant elder in the African Methodist Episcopal Church committed to shepherding, discipling, and enhancing the Christian formation of diverse groups. Zanique is an educator who enjoys teaching in the church or corporate spaces. She is currently enrolled in the PhD program in Christian education at Garrett-Evangelical Theological Seminary.

Rev. Barbara Annette Fears, PhD, is an Assistant Professor of Religious Education at Howard University School of Divinity, where she teaches courses in the history, theory, and practice of ministry. Her research focuses on matters of power, privilege and accountability in spiritual formation, praxis of faith, and curriculum development. She works with local denominations to develop curriculum and is ordained clergy in the United Church of Christ.

Charis Goodman comes from a long line of educators and has been working with children for over thirty years. As both a parent and a kindergarten teacher for the most recent years, she has a passion for early childhood development and spirituality. She is excited to be a part of this incredible work and looks forward to gleaning from the other contributors.

Jenny Haddad Mosher, PhD, serves as Director of Research and Educational Design for the Crossroad Institute of Cambridge, Massachusetts. She is a Palestinian American and Eastern Orthodox Christian and lives with her husband, three young adult sons, and her elderly mother in Durham, Connecticut.

Rev. Tiffany P. Harris-Greene is a minister, writer, and an executive director of a non-profit. Her life is full of adventure and blessings as a wife and mother of three wonderful people. As an avid reader and lifelong learner, Tiffany enjoys documentaries on a variety of subjects.

Rev. Amy Howard is an ordained elder in the United Methodist Church, serving in Alabama. She is passionate about helping people experience the transformational love of Jesus through communities of belonging. Above all though, she loves being "momma" to Cora and Bryson.

Rev. Dr. Jeffrey A. Howard is CEO of The Resource Hub and associate minister at Trinity Baptist Church in Columbia, South Carolina.

Rev. Dr. Denise Janssen is the Associate Research Professor of Christian Education and Assistant Dean for Academics at the Samuel DeWitt Proctor School of Theology at Virginia Union University. She lives in Richmond, Virginia, with her spouse, Rev. Randy Creath.

Rev. Dr. Diane Janssen Hemmen is a PC(USA) minister currently engaged in transitional/interim work with congregations. Her vocational foci have included youth work, systems training and teaching, wider-church leadership, chaplaincy, staff development, and non-profit partnerships.

Erin S. Keyes is an avid learner and teacher. She has devoted her work to marginalized groups of women and children so they can see themselves represented in everyday learning material. Erin shares a home with her loving significant other and two beautiful daughters—she aims to live authentically and out loud, so others feel the freedom to do the same.

Rev. Dr. Virginia A. Lee is the Associate Professor of Christian Education, Director of Deacon Studies, and Director of the Master of Arts in Faith, Culture, and Educational Leadership at Garrett-Evangelical Theological Seminary in Evanston, Illinois. Her primary teaching revolves around child advocacy and centering the voices and experiences of children. She enjoys reading, crocheting, walking, and playing with and learning from her ten great-nieces/nephews.

Dr. Mary A. Love is an adjunct professor in Christian Education at Hood Theological Seminary in Salisbury, North Carolina. She is also a retired editor of church school literature for the African Methodist Episcopal Zion Church.

Colin McDonald serves as the Director of Children's Ministry at First United Methodist Church of Evanston, Illinois, and is a candidate for ordained ministry in the Northern Illinois Conference of the United Methodist Church. He is an avid reader of picture books with (and without) his daughter and wife in their home in Frankfort, Illinois.

Minister Durecia D. Moorer, with a Master of Divinity from Virginia Union University and a Certificate in Youth Ministry and Black Theology from Princeton University, is a distinguished ministry and marketplace leader blending faith, educational acumen, and entrepreneurial spirit to offer invaluable wisdom in cultivating children's spiritual growth.

Hilary Ohrt is a psychiatric and mental health nurse practitioner. She works for a faith-based hospital system, and enjoys helping patients and families of all ages live and thrive despite their mental health struggles.

Evelyn L. Parker, PhD, is Professor Emerita of Practical Theology at Perkins School of Theology, Southern Methodist University.

Rev. Dr. Emily A. Peck is a Visiting Professor of Christian Formation and Young Adult Ministry at Wesley Theological Seminary in Washington, DC. She lives in Maryland with her three children, who keep her on her toes, and their dog, who has ginormous ears.

Rev. Lucas Pepper is an ordained deacon in the United Methodist Church. He currently serves as a middle school special education teacher and is an active union leader. He has previously worked in youth and education ministries within local congregations.

Rev. Rachel Pierce, MA, serves as faith liaison and engagement coordinator for Facts & Faith Friday (FFF) at Virginia Commonwealth University's Massey Comprehensive Cancer Center. She curates conversations and opportunities to connect around science and religion to enhance the lives of people in our communities. She shares her home in Virginia with her partner, Joe, and four children.

Rev. Thomas Rawls has a Master of Divinity from Baptist Theological Seminary at Richmond and a Master of Arts in Christian

Education from the School of Theology at Virginia Union University. He is raising three amazing kids with his wife, Cara. He has served in local church and university settings as a youth minister, campus minister, and associate pastor, and recently started Bigger Table, a home-based faith community in Midlothian, Virginia. Thomas loves coffee, reading, music, woodworking, travel, the Oxford comma, and run-on sentences.

Willa M. Ross is an ordained elder and retired pastor in the Christian Methodist Episcopal Church. She assists in the development of curriculum and discipleship material for the Department of Christian Education and Formation of the CME Church and is editor of *The Practitioner*, a quarterly publication. She is also an adjunct professor at Memphis Theological Seminary. Willa is the mother of three adult children and grandmother of six.

Rev. Dr. Archana Samuel is a dedicated servant of God who served in India as a cross-cultural missionary for fifteen years, and is now serving as a provisional elder in the Virginia Annual Conference of the United Methodist Church in Hampton. She is a first-generation Christian who was born in South India and served God in various places with a variety of gifts and grace. She loves to preach, teach, study, and follow Christ as this is her primary call and vision of life and ministry.

Teresa E. Snorton is the Ecumenical Bishop and Program Development Officer for the Christian Methodist Episcopal Church. She is the Program Administrator for the denomination's Reimagining Children's Ministry project, with extensive experience as a theological educator, a board-certified chaplain and ACPE Educator, and a leader of faith-based non-profit organizations and boards.

Two truths and a lie: **Rev. Justin Thornburg** (they/them) is a parent, death doula, artist, and activist. They have almost been run over by one of the Beatles. They have been a professional wrestling manager. Enjoy life!

Mai-Anh Le Tran is an Associate Professor of Religious Education and Practical Theology at Garrett-Evangelical Theological

Seminary. Her recent research, teaching, and writing trace practical theological understandings of race, violence, the Vietnamese immigrant experience, creativity, and imagination for transformative educational leadership.

Dr. Cheryle Walters Rodriguez is a Christian educator who is passionate about teaching spiritual formation by engaging African indigenous worship traditions toward a more authentic relationship with the Creator. Cheryle enjoys spending time communing with God in nature and supporting her friends, children, and family as they grow in their knowledge of God in their lives.

Rev. Dr. Tamar Wasoian is an independent scholar and religious educator from Syria. She is actively involved in urban ministry, and recently joined the pastoral team at *common cathedral*, an outdoors church for the unhoused in Boston, as associate pastor and program director. Storied learning faith and identity formation are at the core of Tamar's interests and expertise.

Jenna Williams holds a Master of Arts in Education and has worked in K-12 education for the last fifteen years. She is also the mother of three creative, energetic, and active boys.

Rev. Shelley Willmann Weakly (she/her/hers) received her Master of Divinity specializing in Pastoral Care and Counseling at Northern Baptist Theological Seminary. She works as a chaplain at a retirement community. She currently resides in Maryland, where she lives with her husband, youngest son, and two house rabbits.

Bethany Wherry is a decorated educator and proud educational leader. She earned her M.Ed. in Educational Leadership from Winthrop University. Her life mission is to create safe spaces in which children can learn and grow.

Rev. Mary H. Young, EdD, is a recently retired administrator with the Association of Theological Schools in the United States and Canada. She has spent her career as an educator, pastor, and denominational leader. Dr. Young lives in North Chesterfield, Virginia, and currently consults with churches and educational institutions.

Jessica Young Brown is a Licensed Clinical Psychologist and Assistant Professor of Psychology at Virginia Commonwealth University. Her primary interest is in how faith and mental health intersect. She is a mom of two and a lover of belly laughs, kettle corn, and autumn afternoons.

Karen-Marie Yust is Josiah P. & Anne Wilson Rowe Professor of Christian Education at Union Presbyterian Seminary, Richmond, Virginia.